POCKET
GARDENING
GUIDES

WINDOWBOXES

❖

DAVID SQUIRE

POCKET

GARDENING
GUIDES

WINDOWBOXES

❖

DAVID SQUIRE

Illustrated by Vana Haggerty

TIGER BOOKS INTERNATIONAL
LONDON

Designed and conceived by

THE BRIDGEWATER BOOK COMPANY LTD

Art Directed by PETER BRIDGEWATER

Designed by TERRY JEAVONS

Illustrated by VANA HAGGERTY FLS

Edited by MARGOT RICHARDSON

CLB 3378

This edition published in 1994 by

TIGER BOOKS INTERNATIONAL PLC, London

© 1994 Colour Library Books Ltd,

Godalming, Surrey

Printed and bound in Singapore

ISBN 1-85501-387-8

CONTENTS

Early designs	*6–7*
Design factors	*8–9*
Positioning and securing windowboxes	*10–11*
Boxes and troughs	*12–13*
Seasonal philosophy	*14–15*
Choosing the right plants	*16–17*
Colour and design	*18–19*
Red and grey backgrounds	*20–21*
White and dark backgrounds	*22–23*
Winter displays 1	*24–25*
Winter displays 2	*26–27*
Spring displays 1	*28–29*
Spring displays 2	*30–31*
Summer displays 1	*32–33*
Summer displays 2	*34–35*
Summer displays 3	*36–37*
Summer displays 4	*38–39*
Scented windowboxes	*40–41*
Troughs in conservatories	*42–43*
Vegetables and fruits in windowboxes	*44–45*
Herbs in windowboxes	*46–47*
Making a windowbox	*48–49*
Composts and planting	*50–51*
Watering	*52–53*
Keeping plants tidy	*54–55*
Special problems	*56–57*
Pests and diseases	*58–59*
Windowbox calendar	*60–61*
Useful windowbox terms	*62–63*
Index	*64*

EARLY DESIGNS

❖

WINDOWBOXES *capture attention throughout the year: in spring with bulbs and biennials, during summer with brightly-coloured half-hardy annuals and tender perennials, and in autumn and winter with miniature conifers and hardy foliage plants.*

FOR many centuries, in Mediterranean countries and other warm climates, plants in pots have been grown outdoors throughout the year, in clusters on the ground, secured to walls or placed decoratively on window sills.

In London, during the late 1700s and early 1800s, potted plants sold in markets were frequently stood on window sills in summer. People in towns and cities were persuaded to grow plants on window sills and urban gardening societies were encouraged by local clergymen. Speakers were engaged to advise on window sill gardening and competitions for the best displays were widespread. Windowbox enthusiasts were advised to brighten flower pots by painting them red, while less affluent people used tin cans with holes punched in their bases, which were then painted.

The plants used included fuchsias, Mignonette, calceolarias, geraniums, stocks, asters and ericas. Some were bought from established markets, others from street vendors. Unfortunately, those bought from hawkers had a high failure rate: often the plants came straight from warm greenhouses and were not acclimatized to outdoor life.

The compost used in pots stood directly on sunny window sills soon dried out. To counter this, the pot in which the plant was growing was placed inside a large one, and moist moss packed between them. Nowadays, this is known as double-potting and used where the roots and compost of house and greenhouse plants need to be kept cool and moist. Peat is now used instead of moist moss.

Boxes, in which pots could be stood or plants put directly into compost, were a natural progression. Ready-made boxes were available, but home-made ones

BALCONY gardens were highly popular in Victorian times and frequently inspired by extensive displays in Belgium and France. Many balconies in Brussels were like greenhouses, some with miniature stoves and full of tender plants. Others were open and packed with frost-tender plants that were moved indoors or into conservatories in autumn.

were frequently decorated by tacking split hazel shoots into patterns along their sides. An alternative was to secure attractive tiles along their fronts.

Windowbox gardening was closely associated with balcony gardening, where plants were grown in many different containers. Displays on balconies became so large that architects were frequently required to assess the weight problem created by soil and plants.

Miniature balconies were secured around ordinary windows and became known as balconettes. A more lavish and ornate feature was created by adding enclosed glass structures around upper storey windows, while larger and more decorative ones were built around doors at ground level.

WINTER DISPLAYS

As well as growing summer-flowering plants on window sills, winter-brightening arrangements were also created. These were

formed of small conifers (removed when too large), and attractive evergreens and climbers such as ivies that could be trained to create a framework to the display.

Nowadays, there are even more varieties of trailing, variegated ivies that can be used effectively in winter displays.

PLANT *cabinets became popular with Victorian families, each trying to create a larger and more ornate design. Basic ones enclosed windows, while others were built around bay windows, creating what today would be called conservatories. Many were heated with hot-water pipes extended from the kitchen.*

THIS *late Victorian winter display of small conifers and trailing evergreen plants is made more dramatic by training climbers in a loop above the windowbox, unifying the display with the window.*

EGYPTIAN INFLUENCE

Mignonette (Reseda odorata), *a native of Egypt, was widely grown in London windowboxes during the early 1800s, when its sweet fragrance was said to cloak disgusting street odours. This annual was made popular in France by the Empress Josephine, who set the fashion of growing it in pots in window-boxes and indoors.*

DESIGN FACTORS

❖

A VARIETY of materials is used to construct windowboxes and troughs. Although some materials can be used for both purposes, others are best restricted to one. Whatever the materials, do not use windowboxes or troughs larger than 90cm/3ft long (and preferably only 75cm/2¹/₂ft) as longer boxes may break when full. On a wide window sill it is better to use two short windowboxes, as there is then less chance of breakages if they are moved when full of soil and plants.

RANGE OF MATERIALS

• Wood is ideal and windowboxes formed of it can be tailored to suit any width of window sill. Although

soil is often put directly in it, it is better to place a plastic or galvanized metal trough inside. This both protects the wood from water and enables displays to be changed more easily from one season to another. It also helps to keep the compost cool in summer.

• Plastic creates durable windowboxes and troughs if thick and rigid. Although frequently used on its own, plastic is better employed as an inner box for wooden windowboxes.

• Terracotta has a texture and colour that harmonizes with all plants. Either position on strong

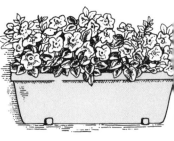

RIGID, *plastic troughs are sometimes used on their own to form windowboxes. Although functional and relatively inexpensive, they do not look as attractive as those with inner and outer boxes.*

GARDENING ON SHELVES

Etagère gardening was introduced from France and gained its name from the French for a series of open shelves, initially used for displaying bric-à-brac. In England it was used both indoors and out to display plants in pots. In many ways it was a forerunner of displaying windowboxes in pairs, one above another on two levels (see opposite page).

ATTRACTIVE *outer, wooden containers into which plastic inner troughs can be placed are the best way to display and grow plants in windowboxes. Seasonal displays can then be changed quickly.*

sills, or use as troughs on patios or tops of low walls.

• <u>Reconstituted stone</u> creates superb troughs for patios, but is too heavy for use in windowboxes except on large, concrete sills.

• <u>Concrete troughs</u> are another possibility, but can only be used on patios, as when large they are extremely heavy.

• <u>Glass fibre</u> is a popular, long-lived material, ideal in troughs and windowboxes.

• <u>Recycled cellulose</u> fibre troughs, although not aesthetically pleasing to all eyes, are ideal as low-cost, short-lived windowboxes or as troughs for putting at the edges of flat roofs to create cascading colour in summer.

TERRACOTTA *creates attractive, firmly based windowboxes and troughs. They are heavy, especially when filled with compost, and therefore when used as windowboxes are best positioned on stone or concrete sills, rather than being held on brackets.*

DOUBLE-LEVEL WINDOWBOXES

Extra colour is easily created by securing one windowbox above another. As well as positioning them under windows, attractive features can be created against long, bland walls. Paint the windowbox to contrast with the wall's colour, and select plants that harmonize with the box and surroundings.

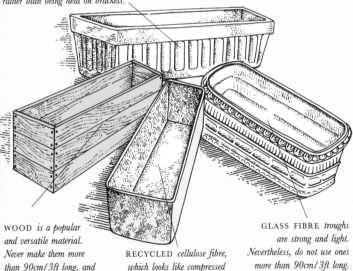

WOOD *is a popular and versatile material. Never make them more than 90cm/3ft long, and preferably only 75cm/2¹/₂ft. If too long, they may break when filled with compost and moved.*

RECYCLED *cellulose fibre, which looks like compressed peat, forms short-lived troughs that are best suited for placing on patios or the edges of flat roofs.*

GLASS FIBRE *troughs are strong and light. Nevertheless, do not use ones more than 90cm/3ft long. They are long-lived and often made in designs that resemble antique containers with detailed patterns.*

POSITIONING AND
SECURING WINDOWBOXES

❖

WINDOWBOXES are obviously associated with windows. But their trough-like design makes them ideal for displaying in other places too. Away from windows they can be used to brighten many places, which are described on pages 12 and 13. When used to decorate windows, however, it is the type of window that influences their positions.

TYPES OF WINDOW

• <u>Sash windows</u> are formed of two areas of glass which can be raised and lowered. This arrangement leaves the sill area uncluttered and with space for windowboxes. Wooden windowboxes with inner plastic troughs are ideal. Alternatively, use terracotta types if the ledge is extremely strong and made of stone or concrete.

Rather than placing windowboxes directly on the sill, position them on 12–18mm/$^1/_2$–$^3/_4$in-square, 15–20cm/6–8in-long, pieces of wood. This ensures that air circulates under the container's base and is especially important when the box or sill is made of wood. Shallow drip-trays also can be used.

Usually, these boxes when filled with compost are quite steady, but in winter, if planted with conifers, they could be badly buffeted by wind. Therefore, secure the windowbox to the wooden framework of the window.

• <u>Casement windows</u> are those hinged at their outer edges and therefore when opened swing out over the sill. This prevents windowboxes being placed on the sill and makes it essential to position them on brackets secured 15–20cm/6–8in below the sill's edge. This distance is influenced by the heights of the plants.

Strong brackets and firm wall fixings are essential (see opposite). Ensure that the brackets have lips at their edges to prevent boxes falling off. This is especially important in windy positions

SASH *windows create ideal homes for windowboxes, enabling plants to be admired from both outside and within. This is especially important when scented plants are used.*

CASEMENT *windows hinge outwards. Therefore, windowboxes must be secured well below the sill, so that flowers and foliage are not damaged when the windows are opened.*

POSITIONING *windowboxes in narrow spaces between symmetrical windows produces an unusual feature. But ensure that the box can be easily watered and looked after.*

PROPRIETARY *brackets to secure windowboxes are readily available. Some brackets protrude underneath, others fit behind.*

HOME-MADE *brackets are easily constructed. Rivet the metal strips together and brace the bracket with a piece of metal at about 45 degrees.*

• <u>Plastic-framed windows</u> have many designs: some are like casements, while others hinge in a cantilever fashion and open out in a wide arch over the sill. Whatever the type, it usually means that the windowbox has to be supported on brackets slightly below the sill.

SECURING THE BRACKETS

Windowboxes secured to walls are usually supported by two brackets screwed into the brickwork and held by masonry fixings. Position the brackets 15–20cm/6–8in (about one-fifth of the box's length) in from each end.

To fix the brackets, measure 15–20cm/6–8in down from the sill, plus the depth of the box. Position one bracket vertically and mark the wall. Use a masonry drill to form holes, then insert wall fixings and use galvanized screws to hold the bracket to the wall. Then, approximately position the other bracket and place a piece of wood across them, with a spirit-level on top. When they are level, mark the wall, drill and plug it and screw the bracket into place.

PARLOUR GARDENING

In Victorian times, indoor gardening became known as parlour gardening. People who were unable to garden outdoors, were encouraged to grow potted plants in troughs.

The design and decorations on these troughs varied according to the rooms in which they were to be placed. Those used in parlours frequently had a rustic appearance, while ones for dining rooms had ornate designs.

A plant box for a parlour

For use in a dining room

BOXES AS TROUGHS

❖

ROUGHS are more versatile than windowboxes and can be displayed in many places. Some of these uses are illustrated here and include the bases of balconies, and on the tops and sides of walls. But there are others to consider.

RANGE OF USES

• <u>Patio edges</u> are soon brightened during summer by planting troughs with bright-faced flowers and positioning them either on low balustrades or directly on a patio's surface. If placed on low walls, use a combination of short, bushy plants and trailing types, so that the wall becomes clothed in colour. However, if the troughs are placed directly on the ground use upright plants.

Placing ground-based troughs on 2.5cm/1in-square strips of wood (or bricks) helps to reduce the risk of slugs and snails attacking plants during warm summer evenings and nights. Soft plants are soon devastated by slugs and snails, sometimes overnight.

WIND FACTOR

Balconies and the tops of walls are often buffeted by winds, so take care not to use too many tall plants. Unless the trough is secured to a wall, it is best just to create a display of frost-tender bedding plants throughout summer. Lysimachia nummularia *'Aurea', the yellow-leaved form of the trailing, herbaceous perennial Creeping Jenny, is ideal for softening the edges of balconies and troughs on walls.*

• <u>Flat roofs</u> on garages and home extensions can be brightened in summer, but avoid blocking gutters. Place troughs planted with trailing plants along the edges. There are many trailing summer-flowering bedding plants to choose from, including forms of lobelia, petunias and impatiens. Place each trough on four or five, 2.5cm/1in-square pieces of wood, and ensure the compost is kept

POSITION *troughs at the edges of balconies, so that trailing plants can cascade through the railings. Place drip-trays under the troughs to prevent water splashing on plants or people below.*

TROUGHS *are ideal for brightening the tops of walls, especially those up to about 75cm/2¹/₂ft high. With high walls there is a risk of troughs falling off and harming people.*

USE *brackets – similar to those employed to secure windowboxes under windows – to hold troughs against walls. These are ideal for brightening high walls. Use bushy and trailing plants.*

moist. During hot summer days, it may be necessary to water several times. Putting moisture-retentive materials such as perlite and vermiculite in compost helps it to retain moisture.

Colour harmonize these plants with their backgrounds (see pages 20 to 23). Putting spring and winter displays in these positions is not practical, as they will be blown about and the compost becomes too wet.

TROUGHS *supported on bricks or on two upright logs inserted into the ground create eye-catching features, in winter as well as throughout summer. In late spring and summer, use slug and snail baits to protect the plants.*

• Summer-houses need brightening in summer. Windowboxes secured under windows are attractive, but also place troughs on verandahs or surrounding areas. Either put drip-trays under the troughs, or place them on bricks, to prevent wood underneath from rotting rapidly.

• Edgese of ponds can be brightened by positioning troughs of bushy and trailing summer-flowering plants around them. Place them on 2.5cm/1in-thick pieces of wood: this enables water to pass underneath and reduces the risk of slugs and snails feasting on the plants. Do not completely encircle a pond in this way, as it may look like a well! However, if the patio edge around a pond is at an uneven height above the water, trailing plants may help to camouflage this. Also, if the liner is tatty or the pond leaks around its edges and therefore exposes large amounts of lining material, the plants help to cloak it.

The edges of raised pots can also be brightened with troughs of plants, but do not encircle them completely. Use trailing plants that camouflage the trough's sides and merge with the pond's edges. Avoid having stems and flowers trailing into the pond, as they soon decay and contaminate the water. And remove troughs in late summer, before the flowers start to fall off in large numbers.

If your pond is plagued with cats sitting on the edges and looking for fish, these troughs help to make it more difficult for them, although not impossible.

CREEPING JENNY

For more than a hundred years, Creeping Jenny (Lysimachia nummularia) *has been widely recommended for growing in pots and for positioning where it can trail. Also known as Creeping Charlie, Moneywort, Herb Twopence, Meadow Runagates and Twopenny Grass, it was widely used to heal wounds. Fresh leaves were bruised, then applied to cuts and abrasions. It was said that hurt or wounded serpents would seek out the plant, which was why it was also sometimes called Serpentaria.*

Creeping Jenny
(Lysimachia
nummularia)

SEASONAL PHILOSOPHY

THE EASIEST way to create a display in a windowbox is just to plant it in spring with a variety of summer-flowering plants. However, apart from being unadventurous, this does not make the best use of a windowbox. Instead, have three inner plastic troughs and rotate them within the same outer windowbox.

• Spring displays: These are planted with bulbs and spring-flowering plants such as wall-flowers in late summer or early autumn and placed in a cool, out-of-the-way, rain-protected position until the bulbs start to flower in spring. Then, the winter display is removed from the outer windowbox and replaced with the spring-flowering one.

As well as spring-flowering bulbs and biennial plants (which are sown in seed-beds outdoors in early summer, grown and planted into containers in autumn), minia-ture conifers and variegated small-leaved ivies can be used to create extra colour. Bulbs to choose include crocuses, Grape Hyacinths (*Muscari armeniacum*), hyacinths and short-stemmed tulips.

HYACINTH MANIA

In 1597 there were only four varieties of what came to be called the Dutch or Common Hyacinth (Hyacinthus orientalis). By 1725 this had increased to more than 2000, but by 1911 had shrunk to no more than 300.

Hyacinths were widely grown in Britain in the 1630s, but it was Holland that led their development with the raising of double-flowered forms. Their introduction was quite by chance: the Dutch bulb grower Pieter Voerhelm had for many years discarded double forms, but when illness interrupted his vigilance one of them remained which later gained his attention.

Double Hyacinth

Spring — *Summer* — *Winter*

Outer windowbox

WINDOWBOXES *can be attractive throughout the year, but they do need three different inner troughs. In autumn, remove the summer display and replace it with a trough planted with a winter display.*

IN LATE *summer or early autumn, plant another trough with bulbs and some spring-flowering plants, so that in spring it can replace the winter display. In early summer, exchange the spring display for a summer one.*

LONDON'S FLOWER SELLERS

From the beginning of the Georgian period, in 1714, more interest was given to decorative gardening, including plants for homes as well as gardens. Town gardening emerged as a leisure activity and many enterprising gardeners started to travel around with barrows or horse-drawn carts offering plants growing in clay pots for sale. These included small conifers and shrubs. Additionally, artificial flowers made of silk, paper and wire were sold by specialists.

• <u>Summer displays:</u> These are mainly formed of frost-tender summer-bedding plants. Geraniums, fuchsias and tuberous-rooted begonias are among other plants that are used. Because these plants are susceptible to low temperatures, the trough cannot be planted until the risk of frost has passed. However, if a greenhouse, sunroom or conservatory is available, these plants can be planted in the inner plastic trough slightly earlier and put into the window-box later, when all risk of frost has passed.

After removing the inner trough which held the spring display, discard the biennial plants but leave the bulbs in the trough until their leaves die down, then move them to borders, around shrubs. Some gardeners leave them in the inner trough for the following season, but to ensure a good display, always plant new bulbs.

• <u>Winter displays:</u> These are placed into the outer windowbox in autumn, after the summer display has finished. Plants such as miniature conifers, winter-flowering heathers and small-leaved variegated ivies are widely used in these displays.

In late winter or early spring, the winter display is removed and replaced with a spring one.

The box holding the winter display is put in a cool, lightly-shaded position, where it can remain throughout summer. Keep the compost moist.

HERBS NEAR KITCHEN DOORS

Many low-growing and bushy herbs are ideal for windowboxes and troughs, especially as they can then be positioned near kitchen doors. Although individual herbs can be planted directly into a trough or window-box, it is better to leave them in separate pots. Chives, Thyme, Marjoram, Tarragon, Welsh Onions, Parsley and Mint are all possibilities (see pages 46 and 47).

CHOOSING THE
RIGHT PLANTS
❖

PART from selecting plants which form attractive combinations, it is essential that when bought they are sturdy, strong and healthy. It is false economy to buy cheap, inferior plants as they never recover to produce attractive displays. This is especially important with plants intended for planting in windowboxes and troughs – as well as tubs, pots, urns and hanging baskets – as the display is concentrated and a few inferior plants can spoil the design for several months.

MANY *summer-flowering half-hardy bedding plants are sold in 'strips', each formed of several young plants. If more are needed, a complete seedtray of them can be bought. These plants are raised from seeds sown in late winter or early spring, and cannot be planted outside until all risk of frost has passed.*

SELECTING PLANTS

Apart from buying healthy, floriferous and vigorous plants (see opposite), there are a few general factors to consider.

• Avoid tall plants, especially those intended for winter displays. Buffeting autumn and winter winds soon devastate displays with tall conifers, especially in windowboxes secured to first-floor window sills. However, tall plants can be used on wind-protected patios.

• To create the 'body' of the display, use compact plants, but avoid creating a flat, uninteresting surface. Some displays have random, varied heights, while others either peak in the middle or, if in a trough positioned with one of its ends towards a corner, have a slightly triangular outline. Most displays, however, have an irregular 'natural' shape.

SMALL *conifers are usually bought in 6–7.5cm/2¹/₂–3in-wide pots. Check that their roots are not constricted through neglect. Also, ensure the compost is moist and the plants do not have bare areas of foliage.*

EARLY *summer-flowering pot plants, such as Cinerarias (Senecio cruentus), are sold in 7.5–13cm/3–5in-wide pots. Complete with their pots they are placed in windowboxes to create colour early in the year.*

VARIEGATED *ivies are also sold in small pots. Usually, there are three plants growing in the same pot, as this creates a bushy and more saleable plant quicker than when only one plant is used.*

DO NOT *buy inferior plants as they never recover and may leave bare gaps in windowboxes and troughs, spoiling the overall display. Do not buy thin, spindly plants, an indication that they have been grown too close together and neglected. Neither buy small plants in relatively large pots, nor large plants in small pots.*

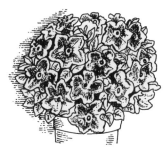

Small plants in large pots may not be properly rooted and established.

Do not buy thin, spindly plants.

WHEN *buying flowering plants in pots for placing in windowboxes to create temporary colour, avoid those that are in full bloom when bought. Such plants will not create a long display. Instead, buy those with masses of flower buds that are just showing colour. Check that the flower buds are evenly arranged around the plant, and not just on one of its sides.*

● Trailing and cascading plants are essential to clothe the fronts and sides of windowboxes and troughs. Use a mixture of those that trail nearly vertically, as well as cascading types which create the impression that the container is larger than it really is.
● Use foliage plants that trail and cascade, in addition to flowering types, as they tend to create a sense of permanency.
● Variegated trailing plants, such as small-leaved ivies and the Variegated Ground Ivy (*Glechoma hederacea* 'Variegata'), create colour in winter, spring and summer arrangements. Small-leaved ivies used indoors can be moved outdoors into containers, but do this in spring so that they have the entire summer in which to become accustomed to the somewhat cooler conditions. They are then better able to survive winters outdoors than if put directly outside in autumn.

CHECK *all plants to ensure they are free from pests and diseases. Small plants are easily checked, but with large ones look both above and under their leaves. Also, check around soft buds and shoot tips. Pests such as greenfly (aphids) breed prolifically if not noticed.*

Inspect the undersides of leaves, as well as their tops.

COLOUR AND DESIGN

During the 1880s, many new plants were introduced into gardens and innovative ways to use them were soon devised. One of these was in formal bedding displays. Later came a less regimated style of using plants, but again an understanding of colour was needed to ensure harmony as well as contrast was created.

Clearly, we are not all pleased by the same colours or combinations of them. Also, not everyone has an accurate perception of colour: up to 8% of males are red-green colour blind. Only 0.4% of women have this affliction. However, by using a colour wheel, selecting colours becomes easier.

USING A COLOUR WHEEL

The philosophy of using colour wheels is that 'complementary' colours (those diametrically opposite) contain no common pigments, while 'harmonizing' ones share the same pigments and are in adjacent segments.

EXPLORING COLOUR

The nature of colour was explored by Sir Isaac Newton in the 1600s when he devised a colour wheel formed of seven colours (red, orange, yellow, green, blue, indigo and violet). Later, the American A. H. Munsell researched colour assessment based on equal changes in the visual spectrum. He created a wheel formed of red, yellow, green, blue and purple, with intermediate colours between them. Colour wheels formed of red, yellow, green and blue were also devised. Another was created from yellow, orange, red, purple, blue and green.

This is at its clearest when only three colours are used to form the wheel: yellow, blue and red. It can then be seen that yellow and violet, blue and orange, red and

TROUGHS *in conservatories can be filled with plants randomly selected and arranged. But when positioned to produce a distinctive outline they can be made to create a feature that highlights the area.*

MODERN *designs with uniform outlines can be produced by using several Mother-in Law's Tongues (Sansevieria trifasciata). For brighter designs, use 'Laurentii' with yellow edges (as above).*

IF A *trough is positioned with one end towards a corner, use a selection of plants to create a tapering display. Put the tallest ones in the part nearest the corner, then graduate the display to trailing types.*

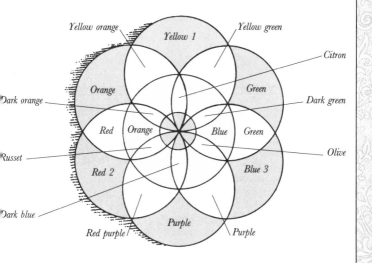

Yellow orange — Yellow 1 — Yellow green

Citron

Dark orange — Orange — Green — Dark green

Red — Orange — Blue — Green

Russet — Olive

Red 2 — Blue 3

Dark blue

Red purple — Purple — Purple

COLOUR *wheels were used in the late 1600s when the English scientist Sir Isaac Newton investigated light and made a wheel formed of seven colours.*

IN THE *late 1800s, the American scientist A. H. Munsell devised a colour wheel with five principal colours, with intermediate ones between them.*

IN VICTORIAN *times, the above colourwheel was featured in the Irish Farmer's Gazette, which arranged the spectrum into six prime colours.*

green are complementary colours, while yellow harmonizes with green and orange, blue with green and violet, and red with orange and violet.

It is the complementary colours that create the greatest contrasts, while the harmonizing ones produce gentle colour associations.

LEAF SURFACES

The surface texture of leaves has a dramatic effect on the perception of colour. Smooth-surfaced leaves reflect light at the same angle at which it reaches them. This creates a purer and clearer light than if reflected from a matt surface. In nature, however, few leaf surfaces are as smooth as glass, and the scattering of reflected light occurs from most of them.

Matt-surfaced leaves harmonize better with flowers than those with dominant shiny surfaces.

INCREASINGLY *in the 1800s, gardening became an accepted pastime for women. Their perception and use of colour is often better than men's and this gave many the confidence to plan its use in both containers and gardens. Towards the middle of the 1800s, many gardening books specially for women were written, notably by Mrs Jane Webb Loudon.*

RED AND GREY
BACKGROUNDS
◆

CHOOSE plants to harmonize or contrast with their backgrounds. It takes only a few moments to plan, and is time well spent. Apart from getting the best from plants, it creates a more unified and attractive display.

The range of background colours can be put into four general groups: red-brick and grey backgrounds are discussed here, while white and dark backgrounds are on pages 22 and 23.

RED-BRICK BACKGROUNDS
These form dominant backgrounds that can overwhelm plants unless used in large clusters. Plants with white, soft blue, silver and lemon flowers form attractive contrasts. Silver-leaved plants are also highlighted by red walls. There are many combinations of plants to suit these positions.
• Spring displays: For sunny positions use the following combinations: light blue forget-me-nots (Myosotis) and white hyacinths; bronze and cream wallflowers

RED-BRICK *backgrounds highlight summer displays of white Marguerites* (Chrysanthemum frutescens), *soft blue flowers (stocks and trailing lobelia), and silver foliage* (Senecio bicolor/S. maritima). *Paint the windowbox white.*

〰〰〰〰〰〰

(Cheiranthus cheiri) and pink and white Daisies *(Bellis perennis)* Grape Hyacinths *(Muscari armeniacum)* and white tulips; variegated small-leaved ivies *(Hedera helix)* Grape Hyacinths and white tulips.

In shaded areas, use a combination of variegated, small-leaved ivies and yellow Polyanthus.
• Summer displays: For sunny positions use white Marguerites *(Chrysanthemum frutescens)*, soft blue stocks, trailing lobelia and the silver foliage of *Senecio bicolor* (also known as *S. maritima)*; trailing Sweet Alyssum *(Alyssum maritimum/ Lobularia maritima)*, soft blue stock and *Senecio bicolor.*

In shaded positions use a combination of light-coloured fuchsias and violas.

GREY STONE BACKGROUNDS
These have a softer and less dominant effect than red-brick walls. Use pink, red, deep blue and deep purple flowers.

MANY *spring-flowering displays are enhanced by red-brick backgrounds, such as white tulips, small-leaved ivies with yellow variegations and the Grape Hyacinth* (Muscari armeniacum).

Spring displays: For sunny posi-tions use boxes entirely packed with wallflowers *(Cheiranthus cheiri)*; deep blue forget-me-nots (Myosotis) and pink tulips; deep blue forget-me-nots and pink or blue hyacinths; a complete display of blue hyacinths.

In shaded positions use Polyanthus, either in one colour to suit the background or a mixture.

Summer displays: For displays in full sun use windowboxes entirely drenched with bushy and trailing pink petunias; lobelia *(Lobelia erinus)* and scarlet gerani-ums (pelargoniums); blue-flowered Star of Bethlehem *(Campanula iso-phylla)* and stocks *(Matthiola incana)*; Petunias, Star of Bethlehem *(Campanula isophylla)*, pink-flowered Ivy-leaved geraniums and red geraniums (pelargoniums); dark blue Heliotrope *(Heliotropium x hybridum)*, red fuchsias and red and yellow varieties of the Basket Begonia (*Begonia* x *tuberhybrida* 'Pendula'). In shaded positions use red or pink fuchsias, Heliotrope or Cherry Pie *(Heliotropium x hybridum)*, begonias and nastur-tiums *(Tropaeolum majus)*.

COMBINATIONS *of red, blue and yellow create attractive features against grey walls. For example, dark blue* Heliotrope (Heliotropium x hybridum), *red fuchsias and red and yellow varieties of the Basket Begonia* (Begonia x hybridum 'Pendula').

GREY-STONE *walls enhance and highlight reds, pinks, deep blues and purple. This summer-flowering display is formed of Petunias, Star of Bethlehem* (Campanula isophylla), *pink-flowered Ivy-leaved Geraniums and red geraniums (pelargoniums).*

CHERRY PIE

Few plants have such an appetite-whetting name as Heliotrope. It is said to have gained its common name Cherry Pie through the scent its flowers emit. However, to many people the sweet, scent is more evocative of embroidery and old slippers. It also has a medicinal use when used to counteract 'clergyman's sore throat'.

The evocative nature of several Victorian varieties may have encouraged gardeners to grow them. Who could resist names such as 'Beauty of the Boudoir' and 'Miss Nightingdale'?

When first introduced from Peru, Heliotropes had washy blue flowers, but nowadays these range from lavender to dark purple.

The plant is said to have gained the name Turnsole because the flowers constantly turn to the sun.

WHITE AND
DARK BACKGROUNDS

❖

W HITE and dark backgrounds are clearly at opposite ends of the spectrum, but they have one element in common – they are both dominant. They therefore need strongly coloured plants in large clusters to create displays. Colours such as bright yellow and red are ideal for white backgrounds, and yellow and white for dark ones.

WHITE BACKGROUNDS

Many houses, especially those with pebble-dashed surfaces, are painted white, creating clinical backgrounds that especially benefit from bright flowers in windowboxes and troughs. Choose mainly yellow, gold, scarlet, red and dark blue flowers, as well as generous amounts of green foliage. There are many plants from which to choose, for both spring and summer displays. Here are a few combinations to consider.
• Spring displays: For sunny positions choose forget-me-nots

AURICULAS

During the 1800s, Auriculas (Primula auricula) *were widely recommended for planting in windowboxes and for window gardening. They were introduced into England in the late 1600s and reached the peak of their popularity about 1850 when miners and silk weavers in northern counties took up their cultivation.*

(Myosotis) and golden wallflowers *(Cheiranthus cheiri)*; Daisies *(Bellis perennis)* and red wallflowers; blue and red hyacinths and crocuses.
• Summer displays: Golden-faced Marigolds, dark red geraniums (pelargoniums) and yellow zinnias, complemented by Emerald Fern

WHITE *backgrounds are ideal for highlighting yellows, reds, scarlets and greens. Here is an arrangement of golden-faced marigolds, dark red geraniums (pelargoniums) and yellow Zinnias. These are complemented by the Emerald Fern* (Asparagus densiflorus 'Sprengeri'). *Paint the windowbox light blue.*

YELLOW, RED AND BLUE *hyacinths look dramatic against white walls and can be accompanied by polyanthus in mixtures of gold, blue and scarlet. Many pansies flower in spring, with colours including yellow, violet and ruby. They contrast superbly with the upright and soldier-like hyacinths.*

DARK *walls create strong contrasts for bright, light colours. To create a semi-formal design in spring and early summer, place three or five Cinerarias in a windowbox (they look better in odd numbers). They are not hardy, so only use them when the risk of frost is low. They are often seen in city windowboxes, where the warmth of buildings gives them protection.*

ALL-YELLOW *windowboxes are dramatic and create beacons of colour when seen against dark backgrounds. Here is a strongly coloured windowbox filled with Creeping Jenny* (Lysimachia nummularia), *yellow Slipper Flowers* (Calceolaria x herbeohybrida) *and tuberous-rooted begonias* (Begonia x tuberhybrida). *For extra colour, use the yellow-leaved Creeping Jenny.*

(Asparagus densiflorus 'Sprengeri'); trailing, red-flowered nasturtiums *(Tropaeolum)*, Iceland Poppies *(Papaver nudicaule)* and yellow Slipper Flowers (Calceolaria x *herbeohybrida*), together with the Emerald Fern; mixtures of geraniums (pelargoniums), Petunias, zinnias, calceolarias and bright-faced marigolds.

DARK BACKGROUNDS

There are probably two types of dark backgrounds, those which are naturally dingy and others that have been planned that way to create a distinctive feature, and could be called 'designer darkness'. Dramatically light colours are needed to brighten them.

- Spring displays: White or yellow hyacinths; hyacinths and yellow crocuses; yellow-variegated small-leaved ivies, hyacinths and crocuses; Cinerarias (in warm positions); bright-faced Polyanthus; white tulips; yellow daffodils (choose one of the low-growing types).

- Summer displays: Creeping Jenny *(Lysimachia nummularia)*, yellow Slipper Flowers *(Calceolaria x herbeohybrida)* and tuberous-rooted begonias *(Begonia x tuberhybrida)*. For extra colour throughout summer use the yellow-leaved form of Creeping Jenny *(Lysimachia nummularia* 'Aurea'); Basket Begonia *(Begonia x tuberhybrida* 'Pendula').

AFRICAN MARIGOLD

Although Tagetes erecta *is widely known as the African Marigold, it originated in Mexico. It was introduced into Spain in the early sixteenth century and became naturalized along the Algerian coast. In 1535, an expedition was mounted to free Tunis from the Moors. The corsairs believed the marigold to be native to Africa and it was reintroduced under the name* Flos Africanus.

WINTER DISPLAYS 1

❖

WINDOWBOXES and troughs can be as interesting during winter as they are in summer. Although at that time of year they are not packed with colour, they can be rich in textures and shades of green, as well as attractively varied in shape.

WHEN TO PLANT THEM

To ensure that winter displays are established by the onset of winter, put the plants in the inner trough during mid to late summer, if they are to be removed from their pots and planted directly into compost. But if the plants are left in their pots, planting can be left until late summer or early autumn (see pages 14 and 15 for seasonal philosophy of planting).

Winter displays can be retained from one year to another and during spring and summer placed in a cool, lightly shaded position. Ensure the trough is slightly raised off the ground to prevent slugs feasting on plants during summer.

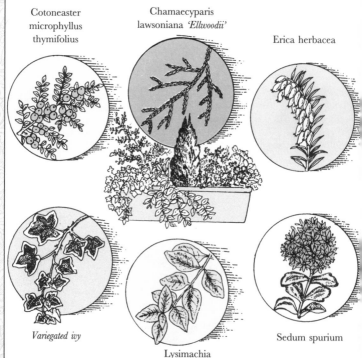

Cotoneaster
microphyllus
thymifolius

Chamaecyparis
lawsoniana *'Ellwoodii'*

Erica herbacea

Variegated ivy

Lysimachia
nummularia *'Aurea'*

Sedum spurium

BRIGHT, *packed window-boxes are especially welcome in winter. They introduce colourful flowers, attractively shaped and textured conifers and variegated trailing plants such as ivies.*

ALTHOUGH *winter windowboxes do not have the colour impact of summer-flowering types, there are many beautiful shades of green and shapes of conifers.*

IN ADDITION *to the colourfully flowered* Erica herbacea *(earlier and popularly known as* E. carnea*), there are some varieties with attractively coloured foliage.*

Hedera helix *'Glacier'*

Hebe x franciscana
'Variegata'

Chamaecyparis
lawsoniana
'Pygmaea Argentea'

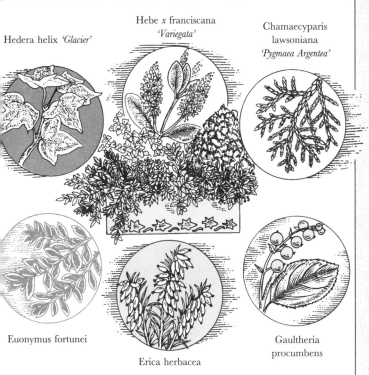

Euonymus fortunei

Erica herbacea

Gaultheria
procumbens

RANGE OF PLANTS

These range from dwarf and slow-growing conifers to variegated shrubs and trailing plants. Eventually, some may become too large for a windowbox or trough. Then, the conifers can be moved into rock gardens, or replanted into large tubs, with trailing plants around them.

The demarcation between late winter and early spring is often uncertain and invariably depends on the climate of your area. Therefore, small, early spring-flowering bulbs can be grown in small pots and put among the more permanent occupants such as conifers. Crocuses are ideal for this, but do not try and force them into producing early flowers.

A wide range of winter brightening plants are illustrated here, and others are featured on pages 26 and 27.

HOUSELEEKS

Houseleeks were recommended during Victorian times for growing in window gardens. They are thought to have gained their name because the Romans grew them in pots in front of their houses. However, the word Leek is said to be derived from the Anglo-Saxon leac, meaning a plant, and therefore a Houseleek is literally a house plant. Its evergreen nature is reflected by its many common names, such as Ayron, Ayegreen and Sengreen, which date back to the fourteenth century. Its other names include Hen-and-Chickens and Old-Man-and-Woman.

WINTER DISPLAYS 2

IN ADDITION to the plants featured here and on pages 24 and 25, there are others to consider:

• *Aucuba japonica* 'Variegata' (Spotted Laurel): Also known as 'Maculata', in gardens it forms a large, evergreen shrub. When young and in a small pot, however, it is ideal for displaying in windowboxes. The glossy, green leaves are splashed with bright yellow and are especially attractive when young. Avoid positions exposed to cold winds, as the leaves then become damaged.

• *Buxus sempervirens* 'Suffruticosa' (Edging Box): A small, hardy evergreen, often used to form miniature hedges around herb gardens. When small and growing in pots it can be used in windowboxes, where the small, dark green and glossy leaves create attractive foils for variegated trailing plants.

• *Euonymus japonicus* 'Microphyllus Variegatus': Dwarf, evergreen shrub with small leaves that reveal

white edges. When young and small it can be grown in pots and placed in winter windowboxes. *E. j.* 'Microphyllus Pulchellus' ('Microphyllus Aureus') has small leaves with golden variegations.

• *Hebe* x *andersonii* 'Variegata': A handsome, evergreen shrub with dull green variegated leaves edged

CHAMAECYPARIS LAW-SONIANA *'Ellwoodii'*: Slow-growing, eventually large conifer with a column-like outline formed of tightly packed, dark green foliage. For extra colour choose 'Ellwood's Pillar'.

CHAMAECYPARIS LAWSONIANA *'Pygmaea Argentea'*: Small, bush-like conifer with bluish-green foliage tipped creamy white. Its shape contrasts with column-shaped conifers: position between them.

CHAMAECYPARIS PISIFERA *'Boulevard'*: Popular, slow-growing, cone-shaped conifer with soft, intense silver-blue foliage. Do not allow the compost to become dry as the foliage will then become unsightly.

JUNIPERUS COMMUNIS
'Compressa': Dwarf and compact conifer with dark green, needle-like, silver-backed leaves set tightly around the plants. It is ideal for windowboxes and troughs, as it only reaches 40cm/16in after ten years.

ERICA HERBACEA:
Earlier known as Erica carnea *and commonly as the Spring or Snow Heather. From late autumn to late spring it creates a mass of colour. Varieties in colours including white, pink and rose-purple.*

EUONYMUS FORTUNEI:
There are many colourfully variegated varieties of this trailing or climbing evergreen shrub. Choose small plants and when they become too large for a windowbox put them into a garden border or large tub.

in creamy white. Eventually it becomes too large for a window-box and can be put into a tub or border.

• *Hedera helix:* This small-leaved ivy has many handsomely variegated forms. Select the brightest ones you can find for winter use, and position at the fronts or sides of the boxes.

• *Vinca minor* 'Variegata' (Variegated Lesser Periwinkle): This grows large, with a trailing and sprawling nature and green and creamy white variegated, evergreen leaves. Eventually it becomes too big for windowboxes and can then be planted into a border. However, when young it is ideal for softening the edges of a variety of containers.

Vincas have been popular camouflaging and ground-covering plants for several centuries, and because of their creeping nature were originally classified as varieties of clematis. Earlier they were known as Joy of the Ground.

CINERARIAS

Earlier known as Cineraria cruenta, *but now as* Senecio cruentus, *this widely grown houseplant is famed for flowers that appear in dome-shaped heads from early winter to early summer.*

The Victorians recommended it for window gardening and in many cities today it can be seen in windowboxes, especially those that are serviced by professional gardeners and florists. Few pot plants create such reliable displays as those produced by Cinerarias, especially at that time of the year.

Cineraria (Senecio cruentus)

SPRING DISPLAYS 1

❖

AS SOON as winter recedes, a wealth of bulbs and biennial plants burst into flower. Exactly when this happens depends on the weather. Some areas seldom have severe frosts and therefore spring could be six or more weeks in advance of exposed areas three to five hundred miles away.

PLANTING A SPRING DISPLAY

These are created by planting bulbs, biennial plants, trailing ivies and small conifers into compost in an inner trough-like container in late summer or early autumn and putting this into a windowbox in early spring. Alternatively, plants can be grown in separate pots and just placed in the trough.

Bulbs such as *Crocus chrysanthus*, *Iris danfordiae*, *Iris reticulata*, daffodils, miniature narcissus, hyacinths and *Tulipa greigii* are all planted when their bulbs become available in late summer or early autumn. The depths to which they

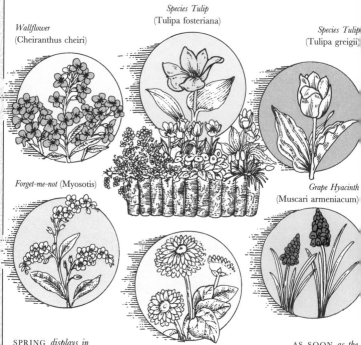

Wallflower
(Cheiranthus cheiri)

Species Tulip
(Tulipa fosteriana)

Species Tulip
(Tulipa greigii)

Forget-me-not (Myosotis)

Grape Hyacinth
(Muscari armeniacum)

Double Daisy
(Bellis perennis)

SPRING *displays in windowboxes and troughs can be a feast of colour, full of bulbous plants such as Grape Hyacinths and short-stemmed species tulips, and biennials like forget-me-nots, Double Daisies and wallflowers.*

THESE *displays need to be planned in midsummer and planted in late summer or early autumn. They are then put in a cool corner.*

AS SOON *as the flowering plants burst into life and create an array of colour, remove the winter display from a windowbox and replace it with the spring one. Keep the compost moist, especially when plants are flowering.*

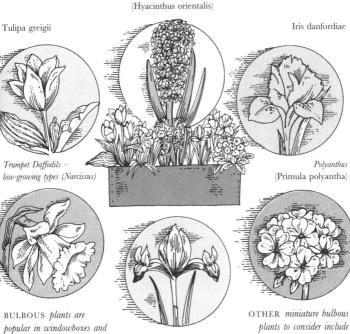

Hyacinths
(Hyacinthus orientalis)

Tulipa greigii

Iris danfordiae

Trumpet Daffodils –
low-growing types (Narcissus)

Polyanthus
(Primula polyantha)

BULBOUS *plants are*
popular in windowboxes and
troughs, but they must be
low-growing. Tall tulips, for
instance, are not suitable,
but many dwarf narcissi
species can be used.

Iris reticulata

OTHER *miniature bulbous*
plants to consider include
crocuses, Grape Hyacinths
(Muscari armeniacum)
and the dainty and
distinctive Iris reticulata
and Iris danfordiae.

are buried vary, but a general indication is to cover them with compost to twice their own depth. For example, a bulb 5cm/2in deep is put in a hole 15cm/6in deep, so that 10cm/4in of compost covers the bulb's top. However, always check with the instruction on the bulb packet.

When planting directly in compost in a container, start by putting conifers at the back and positioning them equally apart. Form clusters of bulbs; tall ones towards the middle and miniature types at the ends and along the front. When using biennials, such as wallflowers, dot them between other plants but behind the bulbs.

Trailers are the last to be planted, at the front.

When planted, gently but thoroughly water the compost and place the container in a cool, sheltered position until the bulbs start to create a display.

POLYANTHUS

These belong to the primula
family and are hybrids between
Primroses (Primula vulgaris)
and Cowslips (P. veris). *They*
are also thought to contain a
dash of P. juliae. *They have a*
perennial nature and each year
create a wealth of colour.

SPRING DISPLAYS 2

❖

IN ADDITION to the plants featured here and on pages 28 and 29, there are others to choose from for spring displays. These include many that are also featured in winter displays, such as miniature conifers, variegated evergreen shrubs and small trailing plants. To enable them to be swapped quickly between seasonal displays they must be planted in their own pots.

LARGE FAMILY

Large, trumpet-type daffodils are well known, but there are many others including miniature ones that are ideal for planting in windowboxes and troughs. The multiflowered Poet's Narcissus (Narcissus poeticus) *develops heads massed with flowers and grows about 38cm/15in high.*

SINGLE-THEME DISPLAYS

Using just one type of plant in a windowbox can create an arresting display. Either use only one colour, or a mixture. For example:
• For a dominant display of yellow, saturate the windowbox with short-stemmed trumpet daffodils. Plant good quality bulbs in an inner trough in late summer or early autumn. Put them in two layers; position the bases of bulbs in the lower layer about 15cm/6in deep, then cover with a thin layer of compost. Position bulbs in the upper layer with their bases between the necks of the lower layer of bulbs.

Fill and firm the trough with compost until 12mm/½in below the rim. Water the compost and

CHEIRANTHUS CHEIRI *(Wallflower): Earlier known as* Erysimum cheiri *and includes dwarf varieties that flower from mid-spring to early summer. They are ideal for growing in windowboxes.*

TULIPA KAUFMANNIANA *(Water-lily Tulip): A distinctive species tulip, with 8cm/3½in-long white flowers, with red and yellow on the outside, during early and mid-spring. Flowers open to a width of about 10cm/4in wide.*

DAFFODILS *with trumpet-like heads create dramatic displays. However, choose short-stemmed types to reduce the risk of damage from strong winds. Plant them in bold groups and position the windowbox in a sheltered area.*

POLYANTHUS *develop large, dome-heads of cream, white, blue, yellow, pink, and scarlet flowers in spring. They grow about 20cm/8in. Plant them in late summer or early autumn. Only a few plants are needed to creat a memorable display.*

NARCISSUS bulbocodium *(Hoop Petticoat Narcissus): Miniature daffodil, up to about 13cm/5in high and with hoop-like, yellow, 2.5cm/1in-long trumpets during late winter and early spring. Plant bulbs in clusters.*

NARCISSUS CYCLAMINEUS *is a miniature daffodil. In windowboxes itflowers in late winter and early spring. It grows 15– 20cm/ 6–8in high, bearing bright yellow flowers with long trumpets and swept back petals.*

place the trough in a cool position until early spring, when the flower buds reveal colour and the trough can be placed in a windowbox.

• The Common Hyacinth *(Hyacinthus orientalis)* develops stiffly upright, soldier-like spires of flowers that, unlike daffodils with their informal outlines, create rigidly-shaped outlines that are ideal where formality is desired. They are also available in a wide colour range – white, yellow, pink, red and blue – that enables more var-

ied colour designs to be produced. Plant the bulbs in late summer or early autumn, with 7.5cm/3in between them and their bases 13–15cm/5–6in deep.

Do not mix different varieties in the same container, as there is then risk that they will not flower at the same time. However, a way to ensure different types flower at the same time is to plant each bulb in an individual pot and at flowering time to select those at the same stage of development.

SCOTTISH ROMANCE

Wallflowers are thought to have been introduced into Britain at the time of the Norman Conquest in the eleventh century. Three centuries later they were found growing on the walls of a Scottish castle. Scott of Tushielaw, son of a border chieftain, fell in love with Elizabeth, daughter of the Earl of March and, disguised as a minstrel, courted her. Her father imprisoned her to deter him, but Elizabeth dropped a piece of wallflower as an encouragement. When trying to elope, she slipped and died, so distressing her suitor that he then wandered throughout Europe, singing and wearing a sprig of wallflower in his cap in memory of his lost love.

Wallflower

SUMMER DISPLAYS 1

❖

S UMMER is the brightest time for windowboxes: they are drenched in colour from when spring displays fade to the onset of frosts in autumn.

The plants are susceptible to damage from low temperatures and therefore cannot be put out-side until all risk of frost has passed. However, when plants are grown in an inner box, they can be planted slightly earlier and at night placed in a greenhouse or conservatory. During daytime, place them outdoors on a warm, wind-sheltered patio. This way, troughs packed with colour can be ready for putting into a window-box as soon as the spring-flowering display fades.

PLANTS TO CONSIDER

In addition to the plants illustrated here and up to pages 39 there are many others, including:
• *Anagallis linifolia* 'Gentian Blue': Growing 15–23cm/6–9in high with a sprawling nature, it develops masses of 12–18mm/

IVY-LEAVED GERANIUMS

These popular trailing plants, correctly called Pelargonium peltatum, *are equally useful in windowboxes as in hanging baskets. When introduced from South Africa to Britain in 1701 they were known as Shield-leaved Geraniums, on account of their leaf-stalks joining the leaves right at their centres.*

$1/2$–$3/4$in-wide, rich blue flowers with bright centres from early to late summer. Plant it where the stems can spread and trail over the container's edges. It colour contrasts with Sweet Alyssum *(Alyssum maritimum/Lobularia maritima)* along the fronts of window-boxes and creates an eye-catching display throughout summer.

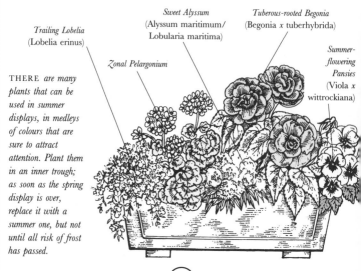

Trailing Lobelia
(Lobelia erinus)

Sweet Alyssum
(Alyssum maritimum/
Lobularia maritima)

Tuberous-rooted Begonia
(Begonia x tuberhybrida)

Zonal Pelargonium

Summer-flowering
Pansies
(Viola x
wittrockiana)

THERE *are many plants that can be used in summer displays, in medleys of colours that are sure to attract attention. Plant them in an inner trough; as soon as the spring display is over, replace it with a summer one, but not until all risk of frost has passed.*

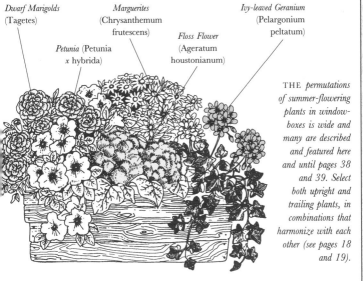

Dwarf Marigolds (Tagetes)

Marguerites (Chrysanthemum frutescens)

Petunia (Petunia x hybrida)

Floss Flower (Ageratum houstonianum)

Ivy-leaved Geranium (Pelargonium peltatum)

THE *permutations of summer-flowering plants in window-boxes is wide and many are described and featured here and until pages 38 and 39. Select both upright and trailing plants, in combinations that harmonize with each other (see pages 18 and 19).*

• *Asparagus densiflorus* 'Sprengeri' (Emerald Fern): A superb cascading foliage plant that is ideal for creating backgrounds for smaller plants. It has long, arching, wiry stems packed with green, needle-like leaves.

• *Coleus blumei* (Flame Nettle): A tender foliage plant widely grown indoors during summer. In warm areas it is also ideal in window-boxes and troughs. Most varieties are upright and bushy, but some have a trailing nature and are ideal for planting at the fronts and sides of windowboxes. Trailing types include 'Scarlet Poncho' and 'Molten Lava'. Both of these can be raised from seeds which should be sown in gentle warmth in late winter or early spring.

• Conifers (miniature and slow-growing types): These are mainly used to create colour in winter and spring displays in window-boxes, but they can also be used in summer arrangements. They are especially useful in exposed and cold areas, as they help to give protection to annual plants.

ZONAL PELARGONIUMS

Although frequently known as bedding geraniums, they are pelargoniums and characterized by having horse-shoe markings on their rounded leaves. In 1710, the shrubby Pelargonium zonale *was introduced into Britain from South Africa and was soon known as* Geranium Africanum. *It became a favourite plant in summer-bedding displays in gardens, as well as for growing in green-houses and conservatories. Later, they were known as Nosegay Geraniums, while in 1863 the first double-flowered form was raised in France. 'Paul Crampel' was introduced in 1903 and has remained popular ever since.*

SUMMER DISPLAYS 2

◆

Fuchsias are popular summer-flowering plants for windowboxes. Although some species are relatively hardy and can be planted in borders in temperate climates, the majority are soon damaged by low temperatures and therefore cannot be put outside until all frosts have ceased.

Some varieties have a cascading nature that soon drenches the sides of windowboxes with colour, while others are bushy. Both have a role to play: trailing types at the ends of windowboxes, bushy ones towards the centre. Avoid varieties with a stiffly upright stance; rather, select those with a lax nature such as 'Lena' (semi-double, pink and magenta) and 'Swingtime' (double, red and milky-white). Trailing types (also suitable for growing in hanging-baskets) include 'Cascade', 'Jack Acland', 'La Campanella' and 'Walsingham'.

PLANTING DISTANCES

Plants in windowboxes and troughs are planted much closer than in flower borders in gardens. This is because colour-drenched windowboxes are essential: if bare patches occur the whole display looks untidy and unappealing, even when the other plants are creating a good show. Therefore, when using these plants in borders, set them further apart than the distances recommended here.

It is possible to plant a windowbox entirely with fuchsias, but companionable plants include Zonal Geraniums (pelargoniums), marigolds, salvias and begonias.

• *Glechoma hederacea* 'Variegata' (Variegated Ground Ivy): Creates a mass of mid-green, kidney-

CALCEOLARIA *x* HERBEOHYBRIDA *(Slipper Flower): Height 20–30cm/8–12in, plant 20–25cm/8–10in apart. It is often grown as a house-plant; outdoors it flowers during early and mid-summer, bearing bright, pouch-like flowers.*

BRACHYCOMBE IBERIDIFOLIA *'Splendour' (Swan River Daisy): Height 23–30cm/9–12in, plant 15–20cm/6–8in apart. Each plant creates a mass of large, daisy-like flowers in blue to purple or white with ebony eyes.*

CAMPANULA CARPATICA *'Bellissimo': Height 15cm/6in, then, trailing plant 20–23cm/ 8–9in apart. Position at the sides and fronts of boxes, so that it covers edges with chalice-shaped, blue or white flowers throughout summer.*

CAMPANULA ISOPHYLLA
*(Star of Bethlehem): Height
15cm/6in, then trailing,
plant 20cm/8in apart.
Superb trailing plant with
masses of blue flowers from
mid to late summer. There
is also an attractive white-
flowered form that looks
good against a red wall.*

CONVOLVULUS
TRICOLOR *'Rose Ensign':
Height 10–15cm/4–6in,
then trailing, plant 20–
23cm/8–9in apart. It
develops masses of rose,
lemon, pink and white,
trumpet-shaped flowers from
mid to late summer. Plant at
the fronts and sides.*

CENTAUREA CYANUS
*'Ultra Dwarf' (Cornflower):
Height 20–30cm/8–12in,
plant 15–23cm/6–9in
apart. It creates neat
mounds of flowers, in
blue or mixed colours,
from early to late summer.
Do not use tall varieties.*

shaped leaves with white markings, in bushy clusters at the
plant's top and then clustered
around long, trailing stems. It is
ideal at the fronts and sides of
windowboxes, as it cloaks them in
leaves without creating a high,
dome-shaped top that obscures
plants at the back.

As a bonus, it has lilac-blue
flowers during late spring and
early summer.

• *Hedera helix* (Ivy): There are
many small-leaved, variegated
varieties that can be used to trail
from around the edges of all types
of windowboxes.

Select the leaf colours to suit
the colour vibrancy of the display.
For example, if the windowbox is
bursting with exceptionally bright
colours, the ivies can be garish.
But when the colours are demure
and reserved, ensure that the ivies
do not dominate the display.
Indeed, these trailing plants
should be secondary features, just
clothing the sides of windowboxes
and softening their outlines.

MORNING GLORY

*When first introduced into
cultivation in the early part of
the 1600s, this tropical
American plant was known
as* Convolvulus major, *then*
Ipomoea purpurea *and
latterly* Pharbitis purpurea.
*Despite all these botanical name
changes it has continued to be
popular and grown as a half-
hardy annual climber in
temperate zones, where it
drenches supports with clusters
of 7.5cm/3in-wide purple
flowers from mid to late summer.
Their colour fades with age.*

*It became known as
Morning Glory
because its
flowers
appeared to
open and to
be at their best
in the mornings.*

SUMMER DISPLAYS 3

EGONIAS are a large and varied family, many ideal for growing in containers on patios, including windowboxes.

• The tuberous-rooted *Begonia* x *tuberhybrida* is dramatic and dominant in windowboxes, with single or double flowers often 13cm/5in or more wide, from early to late summer. Flower colours include yellow, pink, red and scarlet.

They are usually grown from dormant tubers planted in boxes of moist peat in early spring, and later transferred to separate pots when shoots appear. After all the frosts have gone they are planted into windowboxes and other containers outdoors. The Basket Begonia (*Begonia* x *tuberhybrida* 'Pendula') is a trailing form, widely used in hanging baskets and at the sides of windowboxes.

• The fibrous-rooted Wax Begonia *(Begonia semperflorens)* is as much at home in displays indoors as in flower borders outdoors. Also, it is supreme in windowboxes. It forms bushy plants, 15–23cm/6–9in high and wide, with masses of red, pink or white flowers from early to late summer.

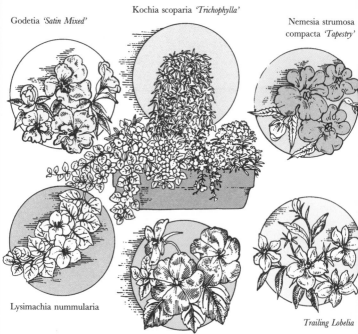

Kochia scoparia *'Trichophylla'*

Godetia *'Satin Mixed'*

Nemesia strumosa compacta *'Tapestry'*

Lysimachia nummularia

Impatiens − Trailing and compact types

Trailing Lobelia

THE *range of plants suitable for growing in windowboxes in summer is much wider than those used for hanging baskets or even tubs on patios. Some are trailing, others bushy.*

WHATEVER *their nature, they must create a colourful display throughout summer, or at least until the onset of late summer.*

MINIATURE *conifers and variegated, evergreen trailing plants are especially useful in exposed and cold areas: they give slight protection to annuals and provide permanent colour.*

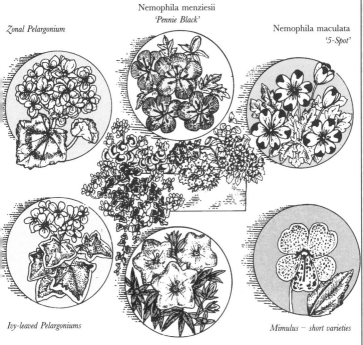

Zonal Pelargonium

Nemophila menziesii
'Pennie Black'

Nemophila maculata
'5-Spot'

Ivy-leaved Pelargoniums

Nierembergia 'Mont Blanc'

Mimulus – short varieties

Wax Begonias are easily raised from seeds sown on the surface of compost in late winter or early spring in 16°C/61°F. Germination takes two to four weeks and when the seedlings are large enough to handle they are pricked out indi-vidually, or in small clusters, into seed-trays. Harden off the plants and put them outdoors when all risk of frost has passed.

Nip out the growing tips of plants several times to encourage them to be much bushier.

NORTH AMERICAN BEAUTIES

Throughout much of the Victorian era, Nemophila maculata *was popular in garden flower beds. It is an attrative, bushy, North American hardy annual. In North America it is commonly known as Five Spot, while in Britain the same name is used as a varietal name.*

The best known nemophila is Baby Blue Eyes (Nemophila menziesii), *with white-centred sky-blue flowers, saucer-shaped and about 30mm/1¹/₄in across. Incidentally, the name Nemophila means grove-lover and was chosen on account of the habitats of many of these species.*

SUMMER DISPLAYS 4

THERE are many more flowering and attractively foliaged plants for planting in windowboxes to create a summer display.

• <u>Heliotropium x hybridum</u> (Heliotrope/Cherry Pie) produces a wealth of flowers, ranging from dark violet through lavender to white. Most plants grow 38–45cm/15–18in high, but in windowboxes lower growing varieties such as 'Dwarf Marine' at 30–35cm/12–14in are better. It has royal purple, fragrant flowers.

Sow seeds 6mm/¼in deep in late winter or early spring and place them in 16°C/61°F. Germination takes two to four weeks. When the seedlings are large enough to handle, transfer them into seed-trays and slowly acclimatize to outdoor temperatures. Plant them into windowboxes when frosts have created, setting them 25cm/10in apart. A few plants will create a dominant feature.

VENERABLE VERBENAS

There are many species of this large South American family, but it is the hybrid Verbena x hybrida *that is the most popular. Its parents were introduced into Europe in the 1820s and 1830s, and within fifty years there were about a hundred varieties.*

• Yellow-leaved Creeping Jenny (<u>Lysimachia nummularia</u> 'Aurea') creates colour through its yellow leaves and bright yellow, cup-shaped flowers that appear during early and mid-summer. It is hardy and increased by dividing established plants in autumn or spring and replanting young shoots from around the outside of the clump.

PANSIES *(Violas): Height 10–15cm/4–6in, plant 10–15cm/4–6in apart. Many varieties to choose from, in mixed and single colours. Ideal for creating vibrant nests of colour, but ensure that they will not dominate other plants.*

PETUNIA *x* hybrida *(Garden Petunia): Height 10–15cm/4–5in – some cascading and ideal for the fronts of boxes, plant 20cm/8in apart. Single or mixed colours, in shades of white, blue, pink, blush, cerise, scarlet and violet.*

SALVIA splendens *(Scarlet Salvia): Height 20–30cm/8–12in – choose low-growing varieties, plant 20–25cm/8–10in apart. Range of varieties in scarlet, deep purple and mixtures. S. s. 'Splendissima' is superb in cool, wet areas.*

SENECIO bicolor *'Silver Dust'* (also known as S. cineraria/S. maritimus): *Height 20–25cm/8–10in, plant 20–25cm/8–10in apart. Forms low mounds of fern-like, silvery leaves. Ideal for creating unusual colour throughout summer.*

TROPAEOLUM majus *'Double Gleam Mixed'* (Nasturtiums): *Height 20–30cm/8–12in, then trailing, plant 15–20cm/6–8in apart. Cascading and trailing, with semi-double flowers in orange, yellow and bright scarlet.*

VERBENA *x* hybrida *(Vervain): Height 20–25cm/8–10in, plant 15–25cm/6–10in apart. Several bushy and trailing varieties to choose from. Plant trailing types at the fronts and sides, with the bushy ones positioned in the centre.*

• *Nicotiana alata* (Tobacco Plant/ Ornamental Tobacco Plant/ Jasmine Tobacco Plant) has sweetly scented flowers from early to late summer. Some varieties are 90cm/3ft tall, but there are several lower-growing types and these are ideal for windowboxes. These include 'Domino F1 Hybrid Mixed' which grows 25–30cm/ 10–12in high with flowers in many colours, and 'Nicki Bright Pink', similarly sized with pink flowers. 'Breakthrough Mixed' is similarly sized, flowering early and with a compact habit. It is tolerant of the heat and therefore ideal in hot climates.

Sow seeds 3mm/¹/₈in deep from late spring to mid-spring, placing them in 16°C/61°F. Germination takes ten to fourteen days. When the seedlings are large enough to handle, transfer them to seed-trays and slowly acclimatize to outdoor conditions. Plant these low-growing varieties about 20cm/8in apart in windowboxes.

VERSATILE NASTURTIUMS

As well as tumbling from windowboxes, many varieties of nasturtium climb and create attractive screens. Indeed, in late Victorian times they were often used to clothe wire-netting screens put around flower beds as protection against rabbits and hares. An essence extracted from nasturtiums was used to spray fruit trees, while many people recommended planting climbing nasturtiums around the trunks of trees to protect them from American Blight, another name for Woolly Aphids, when masses of white, wool-like wax covers shoots.

SCENTED WINDOWBOXES

WINDOWBOXES packed with scented flowers and fragrant foliage are a source of enjoyment throughout the year. Spring and summer are rich in scented flowering plants, while in autumn and winter many small conifers can be relied upon to provide other pleasant fragrances. Here are a few scented flowers that can be grown successfully in windowboxes.

• Common Hyacinth *(Hyacinthus orientalis):* Strongly sweet, especially when windowboxes are completely planted with them.

• Crocus *(Crocus chrysanthus):* Strong and sweet fragrance.

• Flowering Tobacco Plants *(Nicotiana alata):* Use low-growing varieties. Richly sweet flowers.

• Heliotrope *(Heliotropium* x *hybridum):* Fragrance resembles the redolence of cherry pies.

• *Iris danfordiae:* Honey-scented small flowers.

• *Iris reticulata* (Reticulated Iris): Violet bouquet.

'THE PERNICIOUS WEED'

Few plants have such a divisive reputation as Nicotiana tabacum, *the Tobacco Plant and a close relative of the Ornamental Tobacco Plant that is widely planted in gardens and windowboxes. It has generated vast profits for tobacco companies, created massive tax revenues for nations, and contributed to the deaths of many people.*

• Pansies *(Viola* x *wittrockiana):* The cool, sweet fragrance is not particularly noticeable unless they are grown *en masse.*

• Stocks 'Apple Blossom': Double pink and white flowers.

• Sweet Alyssum *(Alyssum maritimum/ Lobularia maritimum):* bouquet of new-mown hay, with a slight honey fragrance.

MINIATURE CONIFERS

The freshness of pine forests is well known, but other evergreen conifers offer surprisingly varied scents when their foliage is bruised. Many miniature conifers that are grown in windowboxes in winter and spring have unusual fragrances, including:

• *Chamaecyparis lawsoniana* 'Ellwoodii': resin and parsley.

• *Chamaecyparis lawsoniana* 'Pygmaea Argentea': resin and parsley.

• *Chamaecyparis pisifera* 'Boulevard': emits a resinous smell.

• *Juniperus communis* 'Compressa': bouquet of apples.

POSITIONING SCENTED WINDOWBOXES

Many of the fragrances given off by flowers are not strong, and therefore they need to be grown en masse. Sometimes this can be achieved by devoting a complete windowbox to them, such as hyacinths in spring. But windowboxes are usually made up with many plants and therefore fragrances become more difficult to detect. Scented windowboxes are best used on ground-floor windows, especially those in warm, sheltered positions.

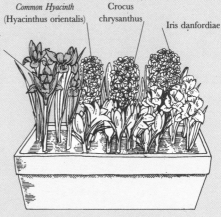

Common Hyacinth
(Hyacinthus orientalis)

Crocus
chrysanthus

Iris danfordiae

Reticulated Iris
(Iris reticulata)

SPRING DISPLAY
*Bulbs are the epitome of
spring, creating bright
flowers, often with the bonus
of rich scents. These include*
Iris reticulata *(violet-
scented)*, Iris danfordiae
(honey-like), Hyacinthus
orientalis *(sweet) and the
diminutive* Crocus
chrysanthus *(sweet)*.

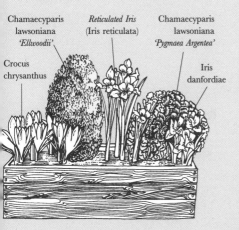

Chamaecyparis
lawsoniana
'Ellwoodii'

Reticulated Iris
(Iris reticulata)

Chamaecyparis
lawsoniana
'Pygmaea Argentea'

Crocus
chrysanthus

Iris
danfordiae

SPRING DISPLAY
*Many conifers have unusual
fragrances.* Chamaecyparis
lawsoniana *'Ellwoodii'
and* Chamaecyparis
lawsoniana *'Pygmaea
Argentea' have foliage which
when crushed emits a bouquet
of resin and parsley. These
can be grown with small,
scented, spring-flowering bulbs
such as* Iris reticulata *and*
Crocus chrysanthus.

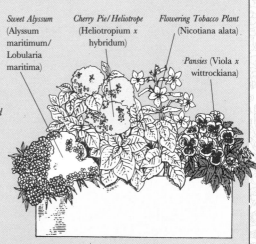

Sweet Alyssum
(Alyssum
maritimum/
Lobularia
maritima)

Cherry Pie/Heliotrope
(Heliotropium x
hybridum)

Flowering Tobacco Plant
(Nicotiana alata)

Pansies (Viola x
wittrockiana)

SUMMER DISPLAY
*Rich medleys of colour and
scent are easily created in
summer. Here is a mixture
of plants that can be increased
from seeds each year.*
Alyssum maritimum/
Lobularia maritima *has
the bouquet of new-mown
hay,* Heliotropium x
hybridum *is like cherry pie,*
Nicotiana *is sweet, while*
Viola x wittrockiana *is
cool and sweet.*

TROUGHS IN CONSERVATORIES

WINDOWBOXES can be secured around the outside walls of conservatories, but ensure the ventilators are not covered and can still be opened. Troughs, however, are ideal for using inside sunrooms and conservatories to display houseplants. Put the flowering types nearer to the windows than those grown primarily for their foliage. Also, plants with variegated leaves need to be put close to the light source.

IN POTS OR PLANTED?

There are two ways of displaying houseplants in troughs in conservatories and sunrooms. Either leave their pots in place and put them on pebbles or a 12–18mm/ $^1/_2$–$^3/_4$in-thick layer of 6mm/$^1/_4$in gravel chippings. Alternatively, remove their pots and plant them directly into peat-based compost.

With both methods, excess water is likely to run out and therefore a drip-tray needs to be incorporated into the design.

The advantage of just placing plants in their pots into a plastic trough is that they can be changed quickly. Also, each plant can be watered individually, so

Pelargonium

Snakeskin Plant (Fittonia argyronera 'Nana')

Dumb Cane (Dieffenbachia maculata)

Rex Begonia (Begonia rex)

Tuberous Begonia (Begonia x tuberhybrida)

Elephant Ear Begonia (Begonia haageana)

CONSERVATORIES *are soon enhanced by house-plants in troughs. Because these plants are left in their pots and just positioned in a trough, displays can be regularly changed as plants stop flowering. Begonias are popular and versatile, some grown for their flowers, others for attractive foliage. There are many beautifully leaved plants, some upright and tall, others bushy, and some trailing.*

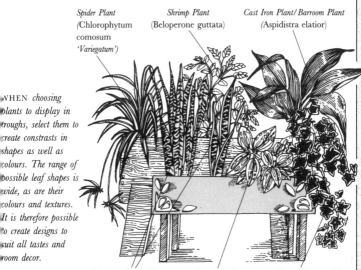

Spider Plant
(Chlorophytum comosum 'Variegatum')

Shrimp Plant
(Beloperone guttata)

Cast Iron Plant/Barroom Plant
(Aspidistra elatior)

WHEN *choosing plants to display in troughs, select them to create contrasts in shapes as well as colours. The range of possible leaf shapes is wide, as are their colours and textures. It is therefore possible to create designs to suit all tastes and room decor.*

Mother-in-Law's Tongue
(Sansevieria trifasciata)

Aluminium Plant
(Pilea cadierei)

Small-leaved Variegated Ivy
(Hedera helix)

that exactly the right amount of moisture is given. It is especially important that flowering plants are left in their pots, as when their display is over they can then be replaced quickly and easily. Plants grown for their attractive foliage can be planted into the trough, as their display lasts much longer. However, when planted all together, it is difficult to ensure each plant is watered properly.

SELECTING PLANTS

Do not use plants that require high temperatures. Although conservatories become very warm during summer, when doors are left open from autumn to late spring, draughts can easily damage tender plants or cause their flowers to fall off.

In addition to the plants illustrated on these pages, there are many other attractive foliage types, including:

• Variegated types: *Aucuba japonica* 'Variegata' (Spotted Laurel); *Begonia masoniana* (Iron Cross Begonia); Coleus (Flame Nettle);

Fatshedera lizei 'Variegata' (Variegated Ivy Tree) and *Hedera canariensis* 'Gloire de Marengo' (Canary Island Ivy).

• All-green types: *Asplenium bulbiferum* (Mother Fern); *Aspidistra elatior* (Cast Iron Plant); *Fatsia japonica* (False Castor Oil Plant); *Nephrolepis exaltata* (Sword Fern).

DUMB CANES

These brightly leaved plants (Dieffenbachias) from tropical America are widely grown in temperate countries as houseplants. Earlier, however, their juice was used by cruel West Indian plantation owners to punish slaves: it is excessively acrid and if stems are chewed causes the mouth to swell, preventing speech for several days.

Medicinally, the roots were used to treat rashes and itching of the skin, while a doctor treating Charles II (1630–85) for dropsy used the plant's juice.

VEGETABLES AND FRUITS IN WINDOWBOXES

❖

STRAWBERRIES and vegetables can be mixed with floral plants in windowboxes, but it is easier to look after them when they are in boxes on their own.

Because windowboxes are positioned about waist height, this gives wheelchair gardeners the opportunity to garden on patios and to grow vegetables and strawberries as well as flowers. Herbs are also a possibility and these are described on pages 46 and 47.

RAISING PLANTS

Many of these plants can be bought from nurseries or garden centres, and if only a few plants are needed this is the best way to start growing them. Alternatively, friends with greenhouses may offer to raise a few plants for you. However, if you want to propagate your own plants, here is the way to tackle the job.

• Tomatoes: Sow seeds 3–6mm/ $^1/_8$–$^1/_4$in deep in early spring and place them in 15–18°C/59–64°F. After germination, slightly lower the temperature. When two pairs of true leaves have formed, transfer the seedlings into individual pots. Slightly lower the temperature and gradually acclimatize the plants to outdoor temperatures. Tomato plants are quickly damaged by frost, so do not plant them outdoors until all risk of frost has passed.

• Cucumbers: Sow seeds singly and 12mm/$^1/_2$in deep in small pots of peat-based compost in early or mid-spring. Place in 20–24°C/68–75°F. After germination, lower the temperature. Keep the compost moist and slowly acclimatize plants to outdoor conditions. Plant into a windowbox when all risk of frost has passed.

• Sweet Peppers: Sow seeds 3–6mm/$^1/_8$–$^1/_4$in deep in early spring and place in 15–18°C/

BUSHY *and cascading tomatoes are the best types for windowboxes. 'Tumbler' is ideal, producing masses of small, cherry-like, succulent fruits. Plant them about 25cm/10in apart. Alternatively, put them at each end of a windowbox.*

COMPACT, *bush-like cucumber plants are ideal in windowboxes. 'Bush Champion' develops 25cm/ 10in-long cucumbers for cutting within two months of being planted in window- boxes. Place them 25– 30cm/10–12in apart.*

SHORT, *globe-shaped radishes, such as 'Juliette', are essential in windowboxes as the compost depth is limited. This variety has crisp, sweet roots with no sign of pithiness, and they grow from marbled sized to very large.*

WINDOWBOXES

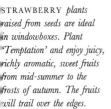

STRAWBERRY *plants raised from seeds are ideal in windowboxes. Plant 'Temptation' and enjoy juicy, richly aromatic, sweet fruits from mid-summer to the frosts of autumn. The fruits will trail over the edges.*

SWEET *peppers are colourful as well as tasty. Grow 'Redskin' in a windowbox in a sunny position. This variety withstands bad weather better than other early sweet pepper varieties.*

LETTUCES *need very little compost, but it must not be allowed to become dry. As a novelty, grow leaf types such as 'Salad Bowl' or 'Red Salad Bowl', which enable individual leaves to be picked over a long period.*

59–64°F. After germination, slightly lower the temperature and when the seedlings have four true leaves transfer them into individual pots, about 7.5cm/3in wide. Lower the temperature, keep the compost moist and acclimatize them to outdoor conditions.

• Leaf Lettuces: Sow seeds in soil blocks or small pots in mid-spring in a cool greenhouse. Put two or three seeds 12mm/½in deep and remove the weakest after germination. Plant into a windowbox in early summer. Seeds can also be sown in shallow drills outdoors and young seedlings transferred to a windowbox. However, there is then a chance that the plants when transplanted will 'bolt' (the premature development of flowers and seeds). High temperatures and dry compost induce bolting.

• Radishes: In early summer, sow seeds 12mm/½in deep in drills formed in compost in a windowbox. Form two rows 10cm/4in apart and when the seedlings are large enough to handle, thin them to 2.5cm/1in apart. The roots can be harvested six to eight weeks after sowing.

• Strawberries: These are traditionally raised by layering runners, but 'Temptation' is increased from seeds. It is best to buy established plants in early summer.

POSSIBILITIES AND LIMITATIONS

Windowboxes usually provide warm, sheltered positions for vegetables and fruits. They are also free from the ravages of slugs and snails, which can rapidly devastate those in gardens.

The plants can be readily reached and looked after, which is essential as the compost must be kept moist but not waterlogged. Indeed, it is the relatively small amount of compost and its tendency to dry out rapidly that is the major limiting factor in windowboxes. Also, supporting plants in these containers is difficult and therefore small, bushy or trailing plants are essential, rather than tall and leafy types. The selection of suitable varieties is paramount.

HERBS IN WINDOWBOXES

N ARRAY of culinary herbs growing near a kitchen door enriches the lives of cooks and creates a welcome range of colourful and attractively-shaped leaves around the bases of windows and in troughs on patios.

Windowboxes and troughs are ideal homes for small, relatively low-growing herbs. Clearly, tall types such as Angelica, Fennel and Caraway are unsuited for growing in this way, but many of them are ideal and are illustrated here. If some become too large, they can be removed easily.

They can be planted directly into compost in an inner, plastic trough that is put into a windowbox, but it is better to leave the plants in their own pots and just to stand them in a windowbox or inner trough. In this way, invasive herbs such as Mint can be restrained. Also, plants that lose their attractiveness can be replaced quickly by younger specimens, or even by other types.

All of the herbs suggested here can be bought direct from nurseries or garden centres as young, established plants.

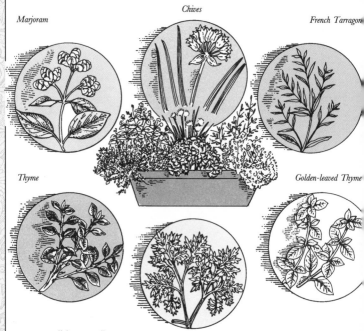

Marjoram

Chives

French Tarragon

Thyme

Golden-leaved Thyme

Parsley

MANY *well-known culinary herbs are suitable for growing in windowboxes and troughs on patios. Ideally, the herbs should be short and not invasive, either through their leaves, stems or roots.*

MINTS *have invasive roots and therefore instead of planting them directly into compost in the windowbox leve them in pots.*

ALTHOUGH *most herbs continue growing from one season to another some, such as Parsley, are raised annually from seeds to ensure the best quality leaves are produced.*

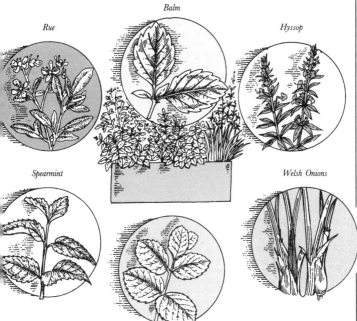

Rue

Balm

Hyssop

Spearmint

Applemint

Welsh Onions

MOST *culinary herbs are primarily grown for their leaves, but some also develop attractive flowers. To encourage the development of young, strong and healthy leaves, flowers are usually removed when young.*

CHIVES *develops attractive, star-like, rose-pink flowers and if left in place create a feast of colour in early and mid-summer.*

PICK *the leaves of herbs when young to encourage the development of further ones. Pinch out the growing tips of young plants to encourage the development of healthy side-shoots. Remove and place them on a compost heap.*

LOOKING AFTER HERBS

Use a windowbox in a warm, sheltered position, preferably facing the sun from mid-morning onwards. In the cycle of using different displays in winter, spring and summer, instead of creating a summer display with floriferous plants, use one of herbs. Then, in autumn replace it with a winter display. This gives the opportunity of using fresh plants every year.

Some of the herbs removed from the display, such as mints, can be divided in spring and used again. Keep the compost moist but not continually saturated. If dry, the plants soon suffer.

MINT JULEP

This cool, refreshing American drink was popular in late Victorian times. It was prepared by putting mint leaves and wine in one glass, and ice into another. The wine and mint leaves were poured into the ice, then back and forth several times. It was further cooled by standing it in a bed of ice, and drunk through a straw.

MAKING A WINDOWBOX

I T IS not difficult to make a windowbox, but it is essential that the wood is cut accurately and squarely. If not, when the parts are assembled, gaps will appear at the joints and it will not be so strong. Use a set square when marking the wood and cut accurately along the lines.

CUTTING THE WOOD
• Sides: Using 18–25mm/³/₄–1in-thick wood, cut two pieces 23cm/9in wide by 75–90cm/2¹/₂–3ft long. Never make a windowbox more than 90cm/3ft long, as when filled it may collapse.
• Base: Again using 18–25mm/³/₄–1in-thick timber, cut a piece 23cm/9in wide and twice the thickness of the wood less in length than the sides. This allows the end pieces to be inset.
• Ends: Using 18–25mm/³/₄–1in-thick timber, cut two pieces 23cm/9in wide and deep.
• Battens: These are needed to secure the sides, base and ends together. Use 2.5cm/1in-square wood, cutting two to the length of the base, and two 15cm/6in long.

ASSEMBLING
THE WINDOWBOX
• Securing the battens: Drill five holes along one side of each of the side pieces. Position the holes 12mm/¹/₂in from the edge. Use a width of drill to suit the galvanized screws, which must be slightly less in length than the combined width of the side and batten. Coat the surfaces with strong, water-resistant glue and screw the side to the batten.

Also, attach two small battens to each of the sides, positioning one end of each of them 2.5cm/1in from the top edge.

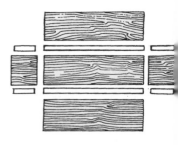

CUT *and space out all the wood needed to construct a windowbox. Check that they are all square and the right sizes. Taking extra care at this stage ensures they will later fit together correctly.*

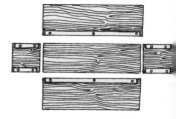

GLUE *and screw the battens to the sides and ends. The battens attached to the sides are for the base to rest on. The ones secured to the ends enable them to be fitted to the sides.*

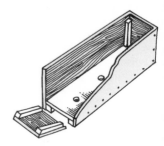

THIS *illustration shows how the windowbox is assembled and the positions of the screws. Use strong, waterproof glue as well as galvanized, countersunk screws.*

MAKING A TROUGH

This design creates a firm-based trough in which tall plants as well as bushy and trailing types can be confidently displayed in conservatories and indoors.

It is basically a wooden trough secured by four stout but ornate legs. The lengths of the legs can suit the location in which the trough is to be displayed. However, troughs more than 60cm/2ft high are likely to topple over, especially if filled with tall, leafy plants.

Use 2.5cm/1in-square pieces of wood to secure the sides and ends together, as well as cross braces at the ends to hold the legs firm and secure.

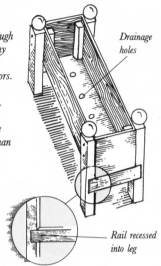

Drainage holes

Rail recessed into leg

- <u>Drainage holes:</u> Before securing the base to the sides, drill five 12mm/$\frac{1}{2}$in holes in it, so that water can drain away freely when the box is in use.
- <u>Assembling the pieces:</u> Stand the sides upright and place the base on top of the battens earlier screwed to the sides. The base must be the thickness of the wood in from the ends, to allow for the end pieces to be flush with the sides. Drill holes and use glue and screws to secure the base to the battens previously screwed to the sides. Then, using the same methods secure the ends.
- <u>Embellishing:</u> Gluing and nailing vertical or horizontal strips of wood to the front of the box makes it look more individual. Keep these simple, rather than too ornate. A veneer of decorative wood can also be used.
- <u>Preparing and painting:</u> When the glue is dry, use coarse then fine sandpaper to smooth the wood. Coat the box in an undercoat and two coats of plant-friendly, non-toxic paint.

MAKING A TROUGH

Troughs are ideal for displaying plants indoors, in sunrooms and conservatories. They are not difficult to construct and are basically formed of a wooden trough on legs. A plastic inner trough can be positioned inside it to prevent the wood becoming damp.

Vertical legs are practical for low troughs, but ensure they are strongly secured to the trough as when filled with plants, legs under stress may fall off. Extra strength can be created in tall troughs by tapering the legs outwards slightly. However, ensure that they do not protrude too far and cause someone to fall over.

In the same way that windowboxes can be given more eye-appeal by securing horizontal or vertical pieces of wood to them, so too can troughs.

Because troughs in conservatories are exposed to high temperatures, and sometimes excessive humidity, ensure they are covered in several coats of paint. This increases their useful life.

COMPOST AND PLANTING

HE NATURE of the compost used in windowboxes is important, as there is relatively little of it and it has to support a large number of plants.

There are two basic types of compost: loam-based and peat-based. Increasingly, other composts are on sale as alternatives for peat-based types. The continual digging of peat from peat-beds destroys the environments of many plants, animals and insects. Several alternatives are available: some made from coirfibre, others from materials such as bark and wood fibre, paper and straw.

• <u>Loam-based composts</u> are traditional composts and formed of loam (good topsoil), peat and sharp sand. The loam must be partially sterilized to kill harmful organisms, and as this is a specialized treatment, the compost is best bought ready mixed. Within the potting mixture range there are several strengths of fertilizer: for plants in windowboxes choose John Innes potting compost No. 2.

Use loam-based compost for winter displays of miniature

PLANTING SEQUENCE

When putting plants directly into compost, start at the front of the box and at one end. First, plant low, trailing types. When these are in place, put the rear row into position, firming compost around them. Ensure the compost of the surface is about 12mm/ 1/2in below the rim, so that plants can be watered properly.

Begin planting at the front

conifers, small shrubs and evergreen trailing plants. Also, this type is good for spring displays of bulbs and biennial plants.

• <u>Peat-based composts</u> are based on peat and are ideal in windowboxes in summer, where it is essential that the compost is able

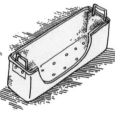

INSTEAD *of putting plants directly into a wooden windowbox, plant them or position their pots in a plastic outer one. This gives the wood a longer life and enables displays to be changed quickly.*

AN ALTERNATIVE *to plastic is galvanized metal. This can be home-made and tailored to fit inside a wooden windowbox. After cutting and folding the metal to shape, use rivets to hold the sides together.*

WHETHER *formed of plastic or metal, the inner trough should fit snugly inside a wooden windowbox, but with a slight space at either end so that fingers can be inserted for easy removal and replacement.*

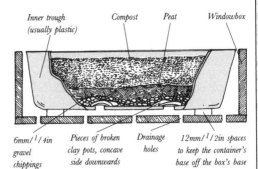

WHEN *planting directly into compost in an inner trough, ensure it is not in immediate contact with the wooden base. Place it on 12mm/¹/2in pieces of wood. As an added precaution to prevent water dripping on people below, place a shallow drip-tray in the base.*

Inner trough (usually plastic) · Compost · Peat · Windowbox

6mm/¹/4in gravel chippings · Pieces of broken clay pots, concave side downwards · Drainage holes · 12mm/¹/2in spaces to keep the container's base off the box's base

to retain plenty of moisture. It is lighter than loam-based composts but does not have such a reserve of plant foods, and therefore regular feeding is essential throughout summer. Also, once dry, peat-types are more difficult than loam-based types to moisten again. Wherever possible, use coir-based or other environmentally friendly composts for planting summer displays.

• <u>Compost additives</u> such as perlite and vermiculite can be used in summer to assist in the retention of moisture.

• <u>Feed plants</u> regularly in summer, using a balanced fertilizer about every two weeks from mid to late summer. Do not use one with a high nitrogen content as this produces lush stems and leaves at the expense of flowers. Moreover, if plants are given too high concentrations of fertilizers there is a risk that they will be irreparably damaged.

PLANTING

Always firm compost around the roots of plants to prevent small air pockets occurring. Unless roots are in close contact with soil particles, their growth is retarded. However, do not pack soil around the plant's neck, so that young stems become bruised and damaged. This can encourage the onset of diseases.

PLUNGING POTS

As an alternative to planting directly into compost, plants can be left in their pots and placed directly in a windowbox or, preferably, first into an inner trough. Ensure the rims of the pots are about 12mm/¹/2in below the top edge of the windowbox. An option is to pack moist peat around the pots to help keep their compost cool and moist. However, never cover the compost in the pots, as the plants in them must be watered individually and the surface compost must be examined to see if water is needed. When the surface is light-coloured and crumbly, further moisture is needed; if dark and slightly shiny, the compost is sufficiently moist.

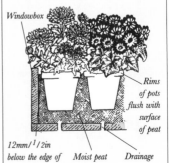

Windowbox

Rims of pots flush with surface of peat

12mm/¹/2in below the edge of the windowbox · Moist peat · Drainage holes

WATERING

KEEPING the compost in windowboxes evenly moist is not easy and requires attention several times a day, in summer if it is not to dry out and the plants to suffer. Compost that is free-draining as well as water retentive is essential. This is achieved by ensuring water can escape from the compost through drainage holes, and using moisture-retentive compost. Additives such as perlite and vermiculite help to retain moisture.

APPLYING WATER

In summer, when windowboxes are packed with flowers, inspect the compost every morning. If the surface is lightly coloured and crumbly, it needs water. If dark, it is probably sufficiently wet. Never let the compost dry out between waterings as it contracts and allows water, when applied, to run

EARLY IRRIGATION

The Egyptians irrigated crops by use of a shaduf (sometimes spelt shadoof) which basically was a bucket pivoted on a counter-balanced pole. A water receptacle was lowered into a river, filled and then swung up and around, and the water poured into an irrigation channel.

Counterbalanced pole

WHERE *windowboxes have large clusters of tubs or pots in front of them use a hosepipe with a 1.2m/4ft-long cane tied to its end. Curve the end of the pipe downwards and apply water in a slow trickle, rather than a sudden jet.*

WINDOWBOXES *at ground-floor level are easily watered with an ordinary watering-can without the rose in place. Do not use an enormous can as it is difficult to lift when full and water then tends to splash everywhere.*

SPECIALLY *designed extensions to hoses are available to enable window-boxes at first-floor level to be watered from ground-level or while standing on a low, firmly secured step ladder. They are also ideal for watering hanging baskets.*

out. If this happens, wait about an hour and apply further water.

Most windowboxes can be watered from outside, but those secured to second-storey windows may have to be watered from inside the room. If this is impossible, special watering lances are available and, combined with a pair of step ladders, watering is usually possible from the outside. Ensure the ladder is stable.

When using a hosepipe, never turn it on full as the jet will damage the compost or blast young plants out of the box. Try not to splash water on flowers and leaves; persistent moistening of them encourages deterioration, and if they are covered with water droplets when the sun is fully out it may cause burning. Therefore, water the plants early in the morning and in the evening, but early enough in late summer so that moisture splashed on leaves is dry by nightfall.

FEEDING AND WATERING

If the plants are being fed, always water the compost first to ensure that the roots of plants will not be damaged by a too strong concentration of plant food. Watering the compost first also enables the fertilizer to spread evenly throughout the compost.

GREEN AT A PRICE

During the latter part of the 1800s watering-pots, as they were then called, were usually made of tinplate and sold in red or green. But as green paint was more expensive, most were red. Those made of zinc were more durable, unpainted and heavier. Later ones were made of galvanized iron, with brass screw roses. There are several designs: some with crescent-shaped, slightly-domed tops which helped to prevent water splashing out when full and being carried. There were two types of handle: those positioned across the can, and others, known as 'Paxtons', running in the direction of the spout. This design enabled the water to be poured with greater ease and precision. The base of each watering-pot stood on three equally-spaced bosses.

Range of Victorian watering-pots

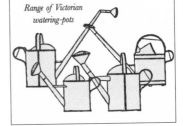

ELIZABETHAN IRRIGATION

The reign of Elizabeth I saw the publication of several gardening books. Thomas Hill wrote a book in 1558 which was enlarged in 1563 and 1577 and became The Gardener's Labyrinth. *He emphasized the importance of water and one illustration showed water being poured into irrigation channels between flower beds. Another book,* The Compleat Gardn'er *in 1693, showed the use of a type of stirrup pump.*

KEEPING PLANTS TIDY

❖

THE DIFFERENCE between a good and an exceptionally attractive display in a windowbox or trough is only a few minutes of careful attention each day. Within a few weeks of being planted, summer-flowering displays are established and creating a radiant array of flowers and leaves. As the summer progresses, flowers fade and stems and leaves often become bent or damaged.

• <u>Removing dead flowers:</u> As soon as flowers fade, pinch them off to encourage the development of others. If left, they can cause the onset of diseases. Where the flowers are borne in large clusters, completely remove the flower stem and always cut them just above a leaf-joint. Short spurs die back and may cause the onset of destructive diseases.

• <u>Creating bushiness:</u> Many plants in windowboxes can be left to create bushy shapes on their own. Others, such as the Wax Begonia *(Begonia semperflorens)*, need to have their growing tips removed

SHOW-TIME CARE

Preparing chrysanthemums for exhibition has always been an art, especially in late Victorian times. Here, special tweezers are being used to 'dress' the flower. Camel-hair brushes were used to remove dust from the petals, while ivory tweezers were preferred to steel ones as there was less chance of bruising the petals.

several times to encourage the development of sideshoots. If this is necessary, always pinch them off immediately above a leaf-joint. Snapping shoots sideways is another way of removing them. Before doing this, water the plants as it is easier to snap stems when they are full of moisture.

REGULARLY *remove faded flowers. Cut off their stems close to a leaf joint. If dead flowers are left on plants, they encourage the development of seeds rather than the formation of further flowers heads.*

NIPPING *out the growing tips of plants encourages the development of sideshoots and creates a bushy plant. Always pinch out the shoot just above a leaf joint, taking care not to leave short pieces of stem on the plant.*

THROUGHOUT *summer, leaves become damaged and unsightly. Smarten up windowboxes either by using a sharp knife or snapping them sideways. Damaged leaves become brown and can be infected with diseases.*

REPLACING OLD PLANTS

Towards the end of summer, some plants may not look at their best. If they are growing in separate pots they can be easily removed and replaced with fresh plants: pot-grown chrysanthemums are good replacements as they remain in flower for several months. If plants are growing directly in compost in the windowbox, they can still be removed and replaced by fresh ones. Take care not to disturb the other plants.

Do not leave shoot tips on the compost, as they encourage the presence of diseases. Instead, place them on a compost heap.

• <u>Damaged leaves and stems:</u> In a garden display, a few broken leaves or damaged shoots sometimes remain unnoticed, but in windowboxes they are easy to see. Remove dead or damaged leaves, either by using a knife or snapping them sideways. Scissors can also be used.

Check the leaves carefully every few days to discover the presence of pests and diseases before they attain epidemic proportions. Pages 58 and 59 provide an idea of the types of pests and diseases that can be expected.

• <u>Replacing damaged plants:</u> This is detailed above and, in preparation for this, each year grow a few spare plants in pots ready for transferring to a container. Alternatively, bright-faced pot plants can be bought throughout summer. And if they are still in flower in late summer, transfer them into conservatories.

Troughs packed with summer-flowering plants can be given an extended lease of life in late summer by moving them into conservatories. Do this before the onset of autumn frosts.

FESTOONING WINDOWS

During the late nineteenth century in England, France, Italy and Spain it was common to festoon windows with climbing plants. Netting, strings and brackets were erected and soon clothed with fast-growing climbers such as Canary Creeper, Morning Glory and Sweet Peas.

SPECIAL PROBLEMS

❖

SOME of the difficulties in growing plants in window-boxes are the same as for hanging baskets and small containers such as urns. These are the relatively small amounts of compost and large number of plants in the container and the difficulty in keeping the compost uniformly moist.

Adding moisture-retentive materials to composts is explained on page 50 and 51, and watering on 52 and 53. Here, however, are a few practical tips to help grow windowbox and trough plants in problem positions.

• Drips from windowboxes: Those positioned at ground-floor level are not a problem, but first-floor ones could drip water over people and plants below unless a shallow drip-tray is used for the inner plastic liner to rest in. However, if the compost contains moisture-retaining additives and is not allowed to become dry between waterings, the risk of

> ### HOLIDAY CARE
>
> *Many displays in containers are ruined by being neglected at holiday times, especially during the peak of summer when compost needs to be watered several times a day. Although water-retaining materials such as perlite and vermiculite can be added to compost, the best way is to ask a gardening friend to attend to them. Ensure watering-cans and hose-pipes are accessible.*

water dripping is practically eliminated. If watering is neglected and the compost becomes dry, it shrinks slightly and when next watered much of the water pours out of the container. Some water will have penetrated the compost and this expands the soil particles, so that when next watered much of it remains.

AVOID *high, wind-swept positions where plants in windowboxes could be battered and damaged. Also, avoid situations where plants cannot be easily watered: at the height of summer the compost often needs watering several times a day.*

CREATE *screens around windowboxes in exposed ground-level positions or on wind-blown roof gardens. Latticework screens are useful as they filter wind rather than creating damaging swirls of air on the leeside of the windowbox.*

DRIP-TRAYS *are essential for troughs in conservatories. Some are positioned within the trough, with the plastic inner trough placed in it. Other trays can be fitted lower down, between the four legs. The latter are usually home-made.*

• <u>Drips from troughs:</u> Those in conservatories can be fitted with shallow drip-trays, either immediately under the trough or lower down. However, troughs positioned on the floor of a balcony might drip water over passers-by. If it is a problem, place a shallow drip-tray underneath.

• <u>Excessively hot positions:</u> Where windowboxes are in exceptionally hot positions it is essential that the windowbox is formed of wood and that there is a plastic inner trough in which the plants are grown. The wooden outer box provides insulation and the space between the wood and plastic also helps to keep the compost cool and to prevent it drying out too quickly, especially in summer.

• <u>Surviving windy positions:</u> Although in windy areas it is possible to erect screens at ground level, it is far better to use low or trailing plants that are less likely to be battered by strong winds.

AVOID USING TALL PLANTS

Although bushy and upright plants are sometimes used in windowboxes secured beneath ground-floor windows, those at first-floor level are best planted with low or trailing types. Pinching out the growing tips of plants helps to make them short, stocky and wind-resistant.

Avoid using tall plants in high windowboxes

Short, bushy plants are wind resistant

POPULAR TROPAEOLUMS

Tropaeolum majus, *widely known as Nasturtium, has been grown in containers for many generations, but* Tropaeolum peltophorum *was equally popular in Victorian times. Here it is seen scrambling and climbing around a balustrade and trailing from a container.*

Tropaeolum peltophorum, *earlier known as* T. lobbianum

• <u>Blackflies:</u> These are especially attracted to Nasturtiums *(Tropaeolum majus)* and often cluster densely around stems and leaves. The blackflies are also tempted by bean plants. Therefore, if your beans normally become infested with these pests, do not grow nasturtiums as invariably they too will become affected.

• <u>Late spring frosts</u> quickly decimate young, summer-flowering plants. Fortunately, most frosts at that time of year are predictable and indicated by a clear sky and little or no wind. Also, warnings of low temperatures are often given by radio and television services.

Placing several layers of newspaper over plants gives them protection from a few degrees of frost, which usually is all that is necessary. Remove the newspaper as soon as the temperature rises.

PESTS AND DISEASES

❖

WINDOWBOXES become packed with soft stems and leaves during summer, creating succulent feasts for pests. Many of these are common and widely seen outdoors, such as aphids (greenflies), while thrips and whiteflies, although also garden problems, are more likely to be noticed on plants displayed in troughs in conservatories.

Crawling pests such as snails, earwigs and woodlice often reach ground-floor windowboxes, but seldom upper storey ones. Dusting insecticides around the bases of

walls helps to control them. Slugs are sometimes a problem to plants in ground-floor windowboxes during wet, warm summers and can be controlled by baits, placed under tiles or pots to keep them dry and away from animals.

Whatever insecticide or fungicide is used, always adhere to the manufacturer's instructions. Increasing the concentration of chemicals is wasteful and may damage plants. Regular spraying at ten to fourteen-day intervals is essential to control infestations of greenflies and whiteflies.

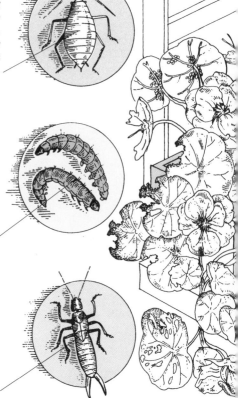

APHIDS (greenflies) suck sap, causing mottling and distortion. Blackflies also infest some windowbox plants, especially nasturtiums. Spray plants every ten to fourteen days throughout summer.

CATERPILLARS chew soft leaves and stems. Pick them off and spray at ten-day intervals with an insecticide. At the end of summer, clear away and burn all rubbish to prevent infestations occurring during the following year.

EARWIGS are pernicious pests, hiding during the day and eating flowers, soft stems and leaves at night. Pick off and destroy them. Also, trap them in inverted pots filled with straw: empty and destroy each morning.

GREY MOULD (botrytis) is a fungal disease that enters plants through cuts and wounds. It is encouraged by damp weather. Remove infected tissue and spray with a general fungicide.

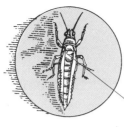

THRIPS are tiny, black insects that especially attack begonias and fuchsias. They cause silvery streaks on leaves and spotting and distortion on flowers. Use an insecticide as soon as the damage is noticed.

VIRUSES infect many plants, causing discolouration and distortion. Leaves may have white streaks. There is no cure: throw away badly infected plants and spray with insecticides to kill pests such as aphids that spread them.

WHITEFLIES are small, white, moth-like insects that spread from plant to plant, sucking sap and exuding honeydew. Check under leaves and spray regularly throughout summer. Plants growing in dry compost are especially badly damaged.

SNAILS often climb walls and ravage soft plants in window-boxes. Pick them off and use baits around the bases of the windowboxes.

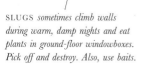

SLUGS sometimes climb walls during warm, damp nights and eat plants in ground-floor windowboxes. Pick off and destroy. Also, use baits.

WOODLICE climb walls and enter windowboxes, hiding in damp places during the day and chewing stems, leaves and roots at night. Dust with gamma-HCH.

WINDOWBOX CALENDAR

SPRING

This is a busy season, especially in areas where late spring is mild and there is little risk of frost.

- In early spring, as soon as bulbous and biennial plants are starting to flower, remove winter displays from window boxes and replace them with spring-flowering types (14–15).
- When planting summer-flowering displays in late spring choose suitable types of plants (14–15).
- There is a wide range of plants for summer-flowering displays in windowboxes (32–39).
- In late spring (in warm areas) remove spring-flowering displays from windowboxes and replace them with summer-flowering ones (14–15).
- When planting summer-flowering displays in late spring (in warm areas), select them to suit their backgrounds. This incurs very little extra trouble and time, but creates a much better and eye-catching display (20–21 and 22–23).
- In late spring, inspect herbs in windowboxes (46–47).
- In warm areas, plant scented summer-flowering windowboxes in late spring (40–41).
- Pinch out the growing tips of plants such as Wax Begonias *(Begonia semperflorens)* to encourage bushiness (54–55).
- When planning summer-flowering displays, always raise more plants than you need, so that they can act as replacements should any die and leave gaps (54–55).
- Late spring frosts can damage plants. Cover them with several sheets of newspaper when frosts are predicted (57).

SUMMER

This is the busiest season for growing plants in windowboxes.

- In early summer (in cold areas) remove spring-flowering displays from windowboxes and replace them with summer-flowering ones (14–15).
- When planting summer-flowering displays in early summer, choose suitable types of plants (14–15).
- Select plants for summer-flowering window-boxes from the wide range (32–39).
- In cold areas, plant scented summer-flowering windowboxes in early summer (40–41).
- When planting summer-flowering displays in early summer (in cold areas), select them to suit their backgrounds (20–21 and 22–23).
- In late summer (in cold areas) remove summer-flowering displays and replace them with winter-flowering ones (14–15).
- Select plants for winter displays with care to ensure they are sufficiently hardy to survive winter (24–25 and 26–27).
- In late summer or early autumn, plant bulbs and biennial plants in an inner windowbox and place in a cool, sheltered position (14–15).
- Carefully select spring-flowering plants for windowboxes (28–29 and 30–31). These are planted in late summer or autumn.
- Plant strawberries and vegetables in windowboxes in early summer (44–45).
- In early summer, inspect herbs in windowboxes (46–47).
- Remove dead flowers (54–55).
- In early summer, pinch out the growing tips of plants to encourage bushiness (54–55).

AUTUMN

If windowboxes are not used for winter displays, remove them from the window, put the compost in a shrub border and thoroughly clean the box with disinfectant. Rinse well and leave exposed to air for about a week to enable fumes to disperse. Then, store under cover until late spring or early summer.

Send away for seed catalogues: they become available in early autumn. Many catalogues have parts specially devoted to plants for growing in windowboxes and other containers. Select a range of bushy and trailing plants. Order seeds early so that you will not be disappointed during late winter or early spring of the following year. If you order too many, they can be stored in a cool, dry, dark place for use the following year.

Geraniums and fuchsias for windowboxes can be bought from specialist nurseries in late spring, so write away now for catalogues.

- In early autumn or late summer, plant bulbs and biennial plants in an inner windowbox and place in a cool, sheltered position on a patio (14–15). Stand the trough on two or three bricks.
- When planting spring displays, select them to suit their backgrounds. This incurs very little extra trouble and time, but creates a much better display (20–21 and 22–23).
- Carefully select spring-flowering plants for windowboxes (28–29 and 30–31).
- In early autumn (in warm areas) remove summer-flowering displays and replace with winter ones (14–15).
- Select plants for winter displays with care, ensuring they are sufficiently hardy to survive winter (24–25 and 26–27).

WINTER

This is the season mainly of waiting and preparing. At this time of year, windowboxes are full of hardy, miniature and slow-growing conifers, small shrubs and evergreen trailers. During winter, do not allow the compost to become saturated with water as this eventually causes plants to deteriorate. However, in warm areas in late winter, growth begins and at this stage the compost must be kept moist.

If there are heavy falls of snow, lightly dust this off plants: if left, its weight may cause damage as well as making the compost too wet when it melts.

In late winter and early spring, many types of half-hardy summer-flowering plants are sown from seeds ordered in autumn or early winter. If you do not have the facilities to sow seeds in gentle warmth it will be necessary to buy them in late spring or early summer. Horticultural societies often sell established plants.

Check brackets that support windowboxes, especially those at second-floor level. Remove and paint them if not in use, and check the wall fixings. If loose, pull them out and replace with new ones. Also, use new, galvanized screws. Ordinary ones may rust, the heads break off and make it difficult to remove them.

During winter, spring displays of bulbs and biennials that were planted in late summer or early autumn need to be checked to ensure the compost is neither saturated with water nor dry. Stand the troughs on bricks to ensure crawling and creeping pests cannot readily get at the plants, especially in spring and in warm areas when the weather is moist.

- In winter, construct windowboxes and troughs (48–49).

USEFUL WINDOWBOX TERMS

◆

APHIDS: *Another name for greenflies or aphis. They suck sap from soft-stemmed plants, causing debilitation as well as spreading viruses from one plant to another.*

BLACKFLIES: *Similar to aphids, but black. They especially attack bean crops in gardens and then spread to other soft-stemmed plants, many that grow in window-boxes and other containers.*

CASCADING: *A gentle sweep downwards, as opposed to trailing when plant stems tumble vertically.*

CASEMENT WINDOW: *A type of window which is secured on vertical hinges and therefore opens out with its bottom edge only slightly above the window sill. With this type of window, it is essential that windowboxes are fitted below the sill.*

COMPOST ADDITIVES: *Materials added to composts to enable them to retain extra moisture – see perlite and vermiculite.*

CONCRETE TROUGHS: *Ideal for positioning on a patio and for growing large as well as trailing plants.*

CORK: *A material used to retain moisture in compost in windowboxes in Victorian times. It was chopped up and added to composts, but it has now been replaced by other moisture-retaining materials such as vermiculite and perlite.*

DEAD-HEADING: *The removal of faded and dead flowers to encourage the development of further ones.*

DOUBLE WINDOWBOXES: *Occasionally, one windowbox is secured beneath another to create a better display of plants. The top windowbox is positioned under a window, with the top of the other one 30–38cm/12–15in below its base.*

DRIP-TRAYS: *Shallow trays sometimes fitted into the bases of windowboxes and troughs to prevent water dripping on people or plants which are below.*

ETAGERE GARDENING: *A type of gardening introduced from France where plants in pots are grown on shelves fitted to a wall, usually indoors but sometimes outside.*

FACE SIDES: *These are the sides of plants that are most attractive. Position plants so that these areas are facing towards the front of a windowbox.*

FROST-TENDER: *Plants that are killed or seriously damaged by exposure to frost. This especially applies to half-hardy annuals in spring, as well as tender perennials.*

FUNGICIDE: *A substance for killing fungal diseases.*

GLASS FIBRE: *Frequently used to make windowboxes and troughs.*

HALF-HARDY ANNUALS: *Tender annuals, raised in gentle warmth in late winter or early spring, slowly acclimatized to outdoor conditions and planted into containers or borders outdoors when all risk of frost has passed.*

HARDENING OFF: *Acclimatizing plants to outdoor conditions. It is especially associated with half-hardy, summer-flowering plants in spring.*

HARMONIZING: *Creating colour-pleasing combinations of plants with their backgrounds.*

INNER TROUGHS: *Usually plastic, sometimes galvanized metal, troughs used to go inside wooden windowboxes to enable spring, summer and winter displays to be changed quickly. They also help to prevent the wood decaying through being continually wet throughout the year.*

INSECTICIDE: *A substance for killing insect pests on plants.*

LOAM-BASED COMPOSTS: *Composts formed of a mixture of loam (good quality topsoil), peat and sharp sand. They do not retain as much moisture as peat-based types, but have a better reserve of plant foods, especially those that are only needed in quite small amounts.*

MASONRY FIXINGS:
Special wall fixings, inserted into holes drilled in walls. Screws can be screwed into them to secure a bracket on which a windowbox can be positioned.

MIXING AND MATCHING: *Arranging plants so that they complement each other and form an attractive feature.*

NIPPING OUT:
Removing the growing tip of a shoot to encourage the development of sideshoots.

PEA-SHINGLE: *Shingle, each piece about 6mm/¹/4in wide. It must be clean.*

PEAT-BASED COMPOSTS: *Compost formed of peat. These retain more moisture than loam-based types and are especially suited for use in windowboxes, where the amount of compost in relation to the number of plants is quite small.*

PERLITE: *A moisture-retentive material added to composts to increase their ability to retain moisture.*

PLASTIC TROUGHS:
Frequently used as inner troughs for wooden window-boxes. Occasionally, however, they are used on their own and positioned on walls or at the edges of balconies. They can also be used at the edges of flat roofs.

RECONSTITUTED STONE: *Frequently used to create windowboxes and large troughs for positioning at ground level.*

RECYCLED CELLULOSE FIBRE:
Occasionally used to create troughs. Ideal for positioning at the edges of flat roofs to create cascading colour throughout summer.

SASH WINDOWS: *A type of window where an area of glass can be raised vertically. With this type, windowboxes can be put directly on the sill.*

SLOW-ACTING FERTILIZERS:
Frequently added to composts in windowboxes and other containers to ensure that plants have an adequate supply of food, especially throughout summer months.

SPACINGS: *Plants in containers are planted closer together than when in borders in gardens. This is to ensure that a spectacular display of flowers is created from early to late summer.*

SPRING DISPLAYS:
These are planted in late summer or early autumn. Bulbs and biennial plants are used to create massed displays of colour in spring.

STOPPING: *Nipping out the growing point of a shoot to encourage the development of sideshoots.*

SUMMER DISPLAYS:
These are planted in late spring or early summer, mainly with summer-flowering bedding plants or tender perennials. These plants are soon damaged by frost and cannot be placed outside until all risk of freezing night temperatures

has passed. At that stage, the trough holding the spring display is removed and replaced with the summer-flowering one.

TENDER PERENNIALS:
Some of these plants, such as geraniums (pelargoniums) and fuchsias, are grown in windowboxes but cannot be put outside until all risk of frost has passed.

TRAILING PLANTS:
Those with stems that trail almost vertically, as opposed to cascading types that have a more arching nature.

VERMICULITE: *A moisture-retentive material added to compost to assist in the retention of water.*

WINDOWBOX: *An open-topped, box-like structure up to 90cm/3ft long and about 23cm/9in deep and wide that is used to create homes for plants. Most are made of wood and, preferably, have an inner plastic or galvanized-metal trough. Other windowboxes are made of materials such as glass fibre and reconstituted stone, but wood is by far the most used material.*

WINTER DISPLAYS:
These create displays from late summer (when summer-flowering plants are killed by low temperatures) to when spring-flowering displays are creating colour. These displays are mainly formed of colourful and interestingly-shaped evergreen plants, although there are several flowering ones. Early-flowering bulbs can also be used.

POCKET GARDENING GUIDES

INDEX

Ageratum houstonianum 33
Aluminium plant 43
Alyssum 20, 32, 40–1
Anagallis linifolia 32
Asparagus densiflorus 22–3, 33
Aspidistra elatior 43
Asplenium 43
Asters 6
Aucuba japonica 26, 43
Auriculas 22

Backgrounds
dark 23
grey 20–1
red 20
white 22–3
Balconies 6–7, 12
Begonia 36–7, 42–3, 54
basket 21, 23, 36
x *tuberhybrida* 15, 23, 32, 36, 42
Bellis perennis 20, 22, 28
Beloperone guttata 43
Box 26
Brachycombe 34
Brackets 10–11, 12
Bulbs 14, 15, 25, 28–31, 40–1

Calceolaria 6, 22, 34
Calendar 60–1
Campanula 21, 34–5
Cascading plants 17, 34, 62
Cast iron plant 43
Cellulose fibre 9, 63
Centaurea cyanus 35
Chamaecyparis 24–6, 40
Cheiranthus cheiri 20, 21, 22, 28, 31
Cherry Pie 21, 38, 40
Chlorophytum 43
Chrysanthemum 20, 33, 55
Cinerarias 16, 23, 27
Climbers 7, 35, 55
Coleus 33, 43
Colour
backgrounds 9, 20–3
design 18–19, 63
Compost 6, 50–1, 62–3
additives 13, 51, 56, 62–3
Concrete 9, 62
Conifers 16, 40–1
spring 28, 30
summer 33, 36
winter 7, 15, 24–5
Conservatories 7, 15, 18, 32, 42–3
Convolvulus 35, 55
Corners 18
Cornflower 35
Cotoneaster 24
Creeping Jenny 12–13, 23–4, 36, 38
Crocuses 14, 22, 23, 25, 28, 40–1

Daffodils 23, 28–30
Daisies 20, 22, 28, 34
Dead-heading 54, 62
Design
colour 9, 18–19
early boxes 6–7
materials 8–9
Dieffenbachia maculata 42–3
Diseases 17, 58–9
Double potting 6, 51
Double-level displays 8, 9, 62
Drip trays 10–12, 42, 56–7, 62
Dumb canes 42–3

Ericas 6, 15, 24–5, 27
Etagere gardens 8, 62
Euonymus 25, 26, 27
Evergreens 7, 25–6, 30

False castor oil plant 43
Fatshedera lizei 43
Fatsia japonica 43
Feeding 51, 53, 63
Ferns 22–3, 33, 43
Fittonia argyronera 42
Flame nettle 33, 43
Flat roofs 12
Floss flower 33
Foliage plants 17, 19, 22, 24–7, 39, 43
Forget-me-nots 20, 21, 22, 28
Fruit 44–5
Fuchsias 6, 15, 20, 21, 34

Galvanised metal 50
Gaultheria procumbens 25, 26–7
Geraniums 6, 15, 21–3, 32–4, 37, 42
Glass fibre 9, 62
Glechoma hederacea 17, 34–5
Glossary 62–3
Godetia 35
Grape hyacinths 14, 20, 28–9, 30
Ground ivy 17, 34–5

Heathers 6, 15, 24–5, 27
Hebe 25, 26–7
Hedera 7, 15–17, 23, 27, 43
helix 17, 20, 25, 27, 35, 43
Heliotrope 21, 38, 40
Herbs 15, 46–7
Houseleeks 25
Houseplants 11, 42–3
Hyacinths 14, 20–3, 28, 30–1, 40–1

Impatiens 36
Iris 28–9, 40–1

Ivies 43
small-leaved 17, 20, 25, 27, 35, 43
trailing 7, 28
variegated 7, 15–17, 23–4

Juniperus 27, 40–1

Kochia scoparia 36

Laurel 26, 43
Lobelia 21, 32, 36
Lobularia 20, 32, 40–1
Lysmachia nummularia 12–13, 23–4, 36, 38

Marguerites 20, 33
Marigolds 22–3, 33, 34
Matthiola 6, 20–1, 40
Mignonette 6, 7
Mimulus 37
Morning glory 35, 55
Mother-in-Law's Tongue 18, 43
Muscari armeniacum 14, 20, 29, 30
Myosotis 20–2, 28

Narcissus 28–9, 30–1
Nasturtiums 21, 22–3, 39, 57
Nemesia strumosa 36
Nemophila 37
Nephrolepsis 43
Nicotiana alata 39–41
Nierembergia 37
Nipping out 54, 57, 63

Pansies 22, 28, 32, 38, 40–1
Papaver 22–3
Parlour gardening 11
Partridge-berry 25–7
Patios 12, 16, 36, 44
Pelargoniums 6, 15, 21–3, 32–4, 37, 42
Periwinkle 27
Pests 17, 24, 45, 57, 58–9, 62
Petunias 21, 23, 33, 38
Pilea cadierei 43
Plant cabinets 7
Planting 14–15, 50–1
distances 34, 63
Plants
choosing 16–17
foliage 17, 19, 22, 24–7, 39, 43
scented 7, 10, 31, 40–1
tidying 54–5
trailing 17, 25, 34–5, 63
Plastic boxes 8, 63
Plunging pots 51
Polyanthus 20, 21, 23, 29, 31
Ponds 13
Primula 22, 29

Reseda odorata 6, 7

Salvias 34, 38
Sansevieria 18, 43
Scented plants 7, 10, 31, 40–1
Seasonal planting 14–15, 24–39
Sedum spurium 24
Senecio 16, 20, 27, 39
Show blooms 54
Shrimp plant 43
Slipper flowers 6, 22–3, 34
Snakeskin plant 42
Spider plant 43
Spring displays 14, 20–3, 28–31, 41, 63
Star of Bethlehem 21, 35
Stocks 6, 20, 21, 40
Stone 9, 63
Summer displays 14–15, 20–3, 32–9, 41, 63
Summer-houses 13
Swan river daisy 34

Tagetes 22–3, 33, 34
Terracotta 8–9, 10
Tobacco plant 39–1
Trailing plants 17, 20, 25, 34–5, 63
Tropaeolum majus 21, 22–3, 39, 57
Troughs 12–13
conservatories 18, 42–3
drip trays 57
indoor 11, 18
making 49
securing 12
Tulips 14, 20, 21, 23, 28–9, 30

Vegetables 44–5
Verbena 38, 39
Vervain 38, 39
Vinca minor 27
Violas 20, 22, 32, 38, 40–1

Wallflowers 20–2, 28, 31
Watering 13, 45, 52–3, 56
Wind 12, 16, 56–7
Windowboxes 6–7, 63
making 48–9
materials 8–9
position 10–11, 40
securing 10–11, 63
size 8, 63
Windows 10, 55, 62–3
Winter displays 7, 15, 24–7, 63
Wooden boxes 8–10, 48

Zinnias 22–3